YOU CAN GET
ARRESTED FOR THAT

YOU CAN GET ARRESTED FOR THAT

2 GUYS, 25 DUMB LAWS,
1 ABSURD AMERICAN CRIME SPREE

RICH SMITH

THREE RIVERS PRESS

NEW YORK

Published in the United States by Three Rivers Press, an imprint of the
Crown Publishing Group, a division of Random House, Inc., New York.
www.crownpublishing.com

THREE RIVERS PRESS and the Tugboat design are registered trademarks of
Random House, Inc.

Originally published in Great Britain by Bantam Press, London.

Library of Congress Cataloging-in-Publication Data
Smith, Rich, 1981–
You can get arrested for that: 2 guys, 25 dumb laws, 1 absurd American
crime spree/Rich Smith. —1st ed.
1. Law—United States—Humor. 2. Law—United States—Anecdotes.
I. Title.
K184.S665 2006
349.73—dc22   2006009267

ISBN-13: 978-0-307-33942-3
ISBN-10: 0-307-33942-4

Printed in the United States of America

Design by Lauren Dong

10 9 8 7 6 5 4

First American Edition

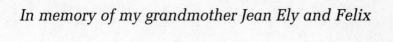

In memory of my grandmother Jean Ely and Felix

Prologue

I am not a man with a criminal history and, by nature, am a law-abiding citizen. The following account, however, would seem to contradict that.

Before the journey I made to write this book, the only criminal act I had ever committed was a speeding offence on the 18th of December, 2001. The Plymouth Fixed Penalty Commission and I exchanged early Christmas presents—I gave them £60 and they endorsed my driving licence with three points.

In the following pages you will witness my twenty-five attempts at breaking laws in America. Unlike many in the country, I wouldn't be murdering anyone, stealing anything, or committing any acts of arson. I felt that, instead, tying giraffes to lampposts seemed a funnier way in which to become a felon.

YOU CAN GET
ARRESTED FOR THAT

ABSOLUTE BALDERDASH

"**A wanghee?** What the hell is a wanghee?"

It was Christmas Day, and I had left my friends in the pub in order to play Balderdash with my eleven-year-old neighbour and his family. Balderdash is like a board game version of *Call My Bluff*, and it's a favourite Yuletide game for my neighbours, the Ellis family. The player acting as quizmaster reads out a question, and the individual players make up plausible answers. The quizmaster selects up to six answers to read out, including the real one. Your aim is to make your fabrication so believable that your opponents select it instead of the real one.

As the game progressed, many of the family members fell by the wayside. Lewis, the eleven-year-old, and his brother, Danny, remained strong competitors, but their mum and grandparents struggled with the ever-increasing pace of the game. You could tell that Linda, Lewis' grandmother, was the most in need of help—her countless shrugs and blank stares were a dead giveaway. Each of her responses was either an unwitting "Oh, the second one" or "I don't know. I'll go for the same as Lisa." These answers always prompted an ardent outcry from Lewis, who was starting to become frustrated at his nan's inability to follow the play. She was sound in mind, but when it really counted—playing board games—she clearly lacked the relevant criteria required for victory.

Lewis was in total charge. He was the youngest player in the game and wanted to win it fairly, and I respected him for his integrity. He was also the most competitive, and as he was just a mere point from victory, he obviously didn't need any favours. I, on the other hand, was five points from being crowned Balderdash champ, and not only did I need to come up with a definition that would fool everybody, but also I would have to choose the true meaning of the word after all the definitions had been read out. This was the most crucial stage in the game, and as Lewis selected a card from the box, he clearly thought that even though he was the designated reader and this turn was probably going to be a non-scoring round for him, his substantial lead couldn't slip—only a miracle would stop him from claiming board game supremacy when it was my turn to play quizmaster.

A wanghee . . . a bloody wanghee? I thought. This made-up definition had to be brilliant—good just wouldn't cut it.

"Hurry up!" shouted Lewis, becoming impatient. He was anxious to get through this round and on to his coronation in the next.

"OK, OK. Hang on. I've almost finished," I replied. I had finished writing, and my definition was believable, I thought. I read it back to myself: *Wanghee: a small South American bird that nests in the fur of other animals*. It sounded good. Very good. I handed it to Lewis and awaited the usual smirk of confirmation that normally followed the reading of the answers. It never came. In fact, my submission was greeted with a slight shake of the head.

What did that mean?

Lewis had played this game many times before, and I was but a Balderdash virgin. Had the definition been used in a previous game that the members of his family were sure to recollect? Was it *so* stupid that not even Linda might choose it?

"A wanghee," Lewis began. "Is it . . ." My heart raced as Lewis read the first four definitions, leaving mine as one of the final two: ". . . Chinese bamboo used for making canes; or a small South American bird that nests in the fur of other animals?"

God, it sounded even better when accompanied by the other definitions.

"Yep. I've heard of that. It's the South American bird." There was an air of certainty about Lisa's response. She sounded so convincing, it was just enough to plant a seed of belief in the minds of the others.

"I'll go for that too," added Cliff, the grandfather.

"Oh, I'll just go with what Lisa said." It was good to hear Linda's trademark one final time.

Lewis looked concerned.

"It might be the bird one," said Danny cautiously. He wasn't about to rush into any decision like the other members of his family. He was cagey and played the game logically. "That bird one's yours, isn't it, Rich?" he asked. He paused and waited for a crack in my poker-faced defence. I remained stoic. In an act of allegiance to his mother's intellect, he proudly declared, "Yeah, I'm going for the bird one too."

"Well, the bird one does sound tempting," I said, trying to hide any signs of ownership. "But the only thing that stops me guessing that is the fact that I wrote it," I added, finally flashing a toothy grin. The hard work had already been done—they had all picked my answer. That meant four points for me, one for each person I had convinced. I now needed only to select the correct definition from the remaining five, in order to gain the fifth point that would take me ahead of Lewis in a crushing upset.

"It's got to be the bamboo," I said to Lewis. "Yeah, I'll go for the bamboo, Lew."

Lewis stared down at the board, clearly counting the number of squares I'd be moving.

"And Rich wins," came Lewis' disappointed drone of congratulation.

"Sorry, mate," I replied sincerely.

I *was* sorry. I felt bad about my success. I had snatched triumph from an eleven-year-old's grasp at the very last second, just when he could taste victory—and on Christmas Day, of all days. I didn't quite know what to say to cheer him up.

Stuff it.

"Winner!" I yelled jubilantly at the top of my lungs, "I can't believe you all fell for it!"

I figured you only get one chance to spoil a young boy's Christmas, so I was going to make the most of it. Lewis knew I was only joking, anyway.

"Yeah, good game, Rich," Lewis said, already sounding as if he'd recovered from his defeat. The boy was competitive, there was no doubt about it, but he was also a good sportsman. He knew he'd been beaten by a better man that day, but he had to be pleased that he'd come so close to beating someone who was twice his age. We chatted as we packed the game away. I started to flick through the box of questions. I remembered one from an earlier round that had intrigued me to such a degree, I hoped to find some similar ones. Like Trivial Pursuit, each card has questions on several topics—in this case it was unknown abbreviations, film titles, people, or (the most bemusing of them all) a completely inane law. Earlier in the game, the Ellises and I had been asked what activity was illegal for divorced women to do in Florida on Sundays. No one's answer even came close to the truth.

"And the real answer is: it is illegal for a divorced woman to go parachuting on a Sunday."

What?

Why?

For the first time that evening, the real answer turned out to be far more ludicrous than any of our manufactured ones.

Divorced women couldn't parachute on Sundays? It simply made no sense. I spent the next few minutes completely distracted from the game, thinking of reasons as to why such a law existed. Maybe women with failed marriages were heavily frowned upon from a reverent viewpoint in the state of Florida, and God wanted nothing to do with them— especially on *his* day, with them being so close to him up in the clouds.

I was sure there was some sort of fabulously esoteric explanation, but in truth the reason for the law's existence didn't intrigue me so much. What fascinated me was the mere fact that such a law existed. The most entertaining country in the world had given me yet another reason to smile.

New Year's passed and 2004 was well under way, but I just couldn't forget about my astonishing Christmas Day discovery. I wanted to learn more. I couldn't merely be content in the knowledge that Florida banned certain people from parachuting on Sunday. I had to know if the law books contained other decrees of a similarly absurd nature.

Modern technology has taught us that the Internet can very often spew out information on whatever you need to know. I was sure that I was just a mouse click or two away from laying my unsettled mind to rest.

A simple online search for "stupid American laws" quickly

led me to DumbLaws.com, a hilarious if vaguely alarming site filled with examples of archaic orders. I clicked on the "American" option and was treated to a fifty-page, state-by-state guide. I was starting to get excited—and by a Web site that didn't feature even a hint of female nudity. Every page brought new laws—there were literally thousands—and a bigger grin of delight to my face.

In Atlanta, Georgia, it is illegal to tie your giraffe to a telephone pole or street lamp; you cannot have an ice cream cone in your back pocket throughout the entire state of Alabama, and it is considered a felony in Arizona if you protect yourself from an intruder with any weapon other than one similar to the trespasser's. I pitied the man who decided on leaving a nine-iron under his bed for protection whilst his would-be burglar chose to break in with a putter.

God, these were good.

I began to wonder just who had been the last person to break the giraffe-tying law. Giraffes aren't even native to America, so I reckoned the only way to breach the ban was to steal one from the local zoo first. One would think that would be the larger infraction. And I'd like to see someone try to smuggle a mammal that size out through the exit doors under his jumper.

After several pages, I seemed to remember most the laws that were either ludicrous or would be rather enjoyable to break. Spitting on the floor of a church featured predominantly in many states, but doing so was neither funny nor farcical and I could see good reason for the law's existence. But a few illegal activities sounded like fun: bowling on the sidewalk was illegal in Chico, California, as was falling asleep in a cheese factory throughout South Dakota.

Could you get arrested for committing these acts? Did the local police even know of their existence? Surely if I was aware that it was against the law to shout "Oh, boy" in Jonesboro, Georgia, the residents must be too. I wanted to know, and I was now seriously considering going to the States to answer these pressing questions. Maybe someone should. Surely this was as good a reason as any to go to America. Wasn't it?

I am no stranger to pointless endeavours. In June 2004 I was bet £20 that I wouldn't "storm" a beach in Normandy on the sixtieth anniversary of the D-Day landings. With June 6 only an hour and a half away, I drove to Dover, boarded a ferry, had my photo taken whilst on the beach, and returned home almost twenty-four hours after I had set off. It cost me £60 to win a third of that amount, and I'd gone a total of forty-two hours without sleep. But the sense of personal achievement I felt more than made up for the financial loss and discomfort. Sod the skeptics—as far as I was concerned, I had accomplished something special.

The next week I travelled to Spain to surprise my neighbours. I arrived on Spanish soil for the first time clutching a scrap of paper with the name of my destination inscribed, and it took me six hours to find their hired villa due to its secluded location in the mountains overlooking the Costa Blanca. But after using nearly every mode of transport available to me, from trams and taxis to a free lift with a delightfully generous lady from Portsmouth, I enjoyed three nights of free accommodation in picturesque Spanish seclusion with the family's two over-the-moon children and their not-so-happy parents. I was sure that I would soon pay for the ordeal I had put them through when we all returned home, but as I slowly sipped a refreshing post-swim drink whilst gazing at the rolling green Spanish hills, I felt victorious again. The bad vibes I had engendered with my flabber-gasted hosts weren't going to dampen my celebratory spirits or the glorious view of the mountainous coast.

My dream of heading to America to break its silly laws esca-lated over the coming days. I was now contemplating not just breaking a few laws but engaging in a daring crime spree—a journey that would take me from one coast of America to the other in a thrilling two-month adventure. I needed a com-panion for a trip of this magnitude.

I knew just the man.

Though Luke Bateman and I are best friends, we had only travelled together once before at this stage—a trip that nei-ther of us would ever forget. A drunken arrangement in the pub one night had landed us in the port of Tallinn two weeks later to watch the 2002 Eurovision Song Contest live in the Estonian capital. Upon arrival, neither of us could re-member why visiting a Baltic nation whilst it was hosting a risible talent contest had seemed like a good idea, but we were fully prepared to make the most of the situation. After declining a kind invitation to purchase a Russian passport and gas mask from an Estonian salesman, Bateman and I vis-ited a brothel that masqueraded as a strip bar/nightclub (the flashing neon light above a secluded cottage should have been a big clue, but I was still shocked when I realised what kind of place I was in), got drunk with a German photogra-pher and a transvestite, and found our three-day holiday was to be extended to four after we missed our connecting flight to Copenhagen due to us passing out on a portside beach at five o'clock in the morning. Yes, Bateman would make a noble accomplice.

My pitch had to be well thought out. Bateman wasn't just

going to agree off the bat to an idea like this. I decided I should ply him with alcohol to the point where he would more or less agree to anything, then get him to sign a watertight contract stating that he would accompany me on such a bizarre adventure. As I drove to his house I had my spiel all figured out. I had thought up answers to all his potential questions and amply prepared for any comeback he may have presented.

"Hiya, Bateman. All right?" I asked as I arrived at his house.

"Yeah." He yawned. "Bit tired, though."

"I've got a great idea," I stated proudly. This wasn't anything new for Bateman to hear me say. Quite often I'd turn up at his house with a crazy agenda for the day's activities.

"Well, I've got to go to the gym at five, so we can't be long," he replied.

"That's OK. I wasn't really thinking about doing something today. This is a bit more long-term."

This was it. No more small talk. It was time to use all my guile and chicanery to sway my friend.

"Um . . . how would you like to go to America sometime and break some laws?" I thought that hat was well put.

"What?" Bateman looked nonplussed.

"There are loads of stupid laws we can break. We could turn it into a road trip . . ." I began to lose steam as I heard the absurdity of what I was saying, "It'll be great!"

Bateman just laughed softly. "Why are we going to do this?"

"Because . . . um . . . I think you and I will have a great time filming it. We could try to get a TV series out of it or something."

"Yeah. Go on, then. I've got nothing better to do. When we gonna go?"

"Next summer?"

"Yeah. OK."

That was it? Was that all it took? Bateman was in. This whole trip was beginning to come together nicely.

I wonder if Guy Fawkes and the rest of the Gunpowder conspirators had been just as easy to recruit.

Over the following months, I began to reveal my plans of an American crime spree to friends. My neighbours thought it was a great idea as long as they were featured in the book. Invariably, everyone I talked to, young or old, thought it was a fantastic plan: "smashing," "excellent," "cool." Were they mad? Not one person I had spoken to labelled it "unrewarding" or "wasteful." They agreed it was "stupid" and "pointless," but I knew that already. Everyone seemed to believe wholeheartedly in the spree, and in me. If I had any doubts that I would do this, they soon diminished after hearing the encouragement from friends and well-wishers. Living vicariously, I suppose.

Bateman and I weren't prepared to attach a giraffe to a lamppost or wait to be attacked by an intruder, but we had found about forty laws that we wanted to break. That was our goal. I looked at a map and realised this was to be a journey of epic proportions, taking us cross-country from the liberal, laid-back surroundings of San Francisco on America's Pacific coast, over the rugged, diverse terrain of mountainous Colorado and Utah, through the country's Midwest, along the Atlantic coast in Florida and South Carolina, and finally to the culmination of the venture in the Northeast near Boston and Rhode Island—A trip of well over 10,000 miles. To me, the beauty of it all was that the majority of the lawbreaking would take place in small towns and cities. I'd noticed, from previous experience, that these small backwaters are where the true characters live, where the people are closer and the atmosphere is friendlier, and where the cogs of the country really turn.

Once upon a time, the prospect of embarrassment and possible incarceration might have daunted Bateman and me, but no longer. Our hearts were set on this journey; our time had arrived. This was our chance to do something we could take pride in and boast of to friends and grandchildren alike. Bateman and I were going to America, and we were ready for anything.

As they say in America, "Bring it on."

And so they did.

2

A good few months had passed, and although we had not yet purchased our tickets to the States, it was clear in my and Bateman's minds that we would spend the majority of the summer over there, regardless of the massive credit card bills we would run up and the wrath we would incur from our respective employers.

Then there was the minor technicality of finishing college. Luckily, the first year of my journalism degree would end a month before we left, giving me a clear three months on holiday before the course resumed in the autumn.

In order to graduate, though, the relevant coursework had to be accompanied by something no person over the age of fifteen ever wants to hear—work experience. The mere mention of the words *work* and *experience* together injects fear and loathing into the hearts of anyone, like me, who had already worked full time for many years and didn't think too highly of the entire concept. Though I hadn't really explained this to the college, I actually wanted to be a teacher. For that, I needed a degree, though what type of degree was never specified. I chose journalism for the sole reason that it was the closest to my house. I now had to find a journalism "job" that would last the week required for course credit. It all seemed like a bit of a waste of time. Besides, how could journalism possibly live up to the week's work experience I served at my local leisure centre a year before my end of school exams? I spent five days either watching the opening-group soccer games of Euro '96 (and occasionally checking members' passes), or attempting to avenge my earlier defeat in the week on the badminton court against a highly skilled member of the over-sixty badminton club who looked distinctively like the comedian Ernie Wise. It was easy, it was fun, and it didn't teach me anything I needed to learn in order to aid my future employment search in the slightest. That was my idea of good "work experience."

Eventually I admitted to myself that sooner or later I would have to comply with the course structure if I was to pass the first year. Luckily, I had a plan. I was glad I knew someone who could help me out without expecting me to do very much.

David Green was the editor of the local edition of our regional newspaper, the *West Briton,* and agreed to take me on for the week. On Monday he warned me of how dull I might find the following five days.

"That doesn't bother me, David," I said sincerely. "As long as you sign the piece of paper that says that I was here, I'll be happy." I envisioned a pleasant week of making coffee and twiddling my thumbs. "What shall I do first?"

David perused his diary, flicking through randomly assorted Post-it notes and indecipherable scribblings.

"There you go." David handed me a small scrap of paper. "Ring this lady, get a quote, and write a story about the senior citizens' party she organised." David's warning had instantly manifested itself into reality. The story I wrote was as thrilling as the quote I found to accompany it: "They had roast beef with all the trimmings and it all went well." Hold the front page.

As the week progressed, I visited the opening of a factory, made a Mother Goose production sound tenuously exciting in text, and appeared at the media table to witness the monthly Kerrier District Council Planning Committee meeting. I only stayed for the first three hours of the meeting, which eventually lasted a further five. The cogs of local democracy appear to turn at an excruciatingly slow pace.

When I returned to the office on Wednesday, I thought I would enliven the deathly quiet atmosphere of the newsroom (well, the only room) by regaling David with an account of my proposed trip to the States in the summer. David didn't look as if he was listening and continued to check the story he had just written for clarity and errors. I continued regardless, and after explaining everything that was pertinent, I sat back and awaited his response.

David relaxed into his chair and removed the biro from between his lips. "You're seriously going to do this?" he asked with a glint of approval in his eye.

"Yeah, why not? Should be fun," I replied wholeheartedly.

"Well, in that case, I think it'll make a great feature for next week's paper. Can you manage about six hundred words?"

Six hundred words? He'd only allocated the senior citizens' party fifty—that made me at least twelve times more important than them, I reckoned. As far as the *West Briton* and local newspapers go, this was a scoop.

It only then occurred to me that my name would appear as the reporter. Would it look slightly arrogant that someone had composed a story about himself?

"Do I have to put my name as the author, Dave?" I asked cautiously.

"Of course you do. Who else wrote it?"

I decided to reword the original question.

"But does *my* name have to be on it? It's my story, so surely I'm entitled to use a pseudonym, aren't I?"

David looked intrigued. "What kind of name were you thinking of, then?"

"Chris Mardith. It's an anagram of Richard Smith. Clever, hey?" I was certainly proud of it.

In almost no time at all, the name received a thumbs-up, the story was written, a mug-shot-style picture had been taken, and my week in journalism had come to an end. The five days of 10 a.m. starts, one-hour lunch breaks, and 2 p.m. departures had taken their toll. I was glad to get away from the hectic schedule and return to my lazy lifestyle.

It wasn't until the following Thursday that I could open the paper and see my story in its entirety, adorning half a page with an accompanying picture. Apart from a few shortened quotes, the story was more or less word for word what I had originally written. I was proud of my accomplishment of appearing in a newspaper without having to fall through a window and lacerate my arm, as I'd done a few years previously. The only reservation I had about the story was the choice of headline the sub-editor had selected: "Mission to Get on the U.S. 'Most Wanted' list." That didn't really convey the true sentiment of my trip. It wasn't my ambition to feature on that list at all. Breaking silly laws was one thing, but in order to rub shoulders with the ten most ruthless felons in America I would have to knock Robert William Fisher off the list by committing a more heinous crime than his triple homicide and arson of an occupied building.

Any concerns soon faded after a few of my friends commented on the story the day of issue. I felt like a minor celebrity in my little north-coast Cornish village.

That evening I received a call from a man by the name of

Sam. Sam worked for the press agency in Plymouth and it was his job to scour all the region's newspapers for stories in which the nationals might show an interest. I pitied him instantly.

"I'm not promising anything, Richard. But a national or two may pick it up, I really don't know." Sam seemed very uncertain, but I didn't care; it was all a bit of a novelty anyway.

"Do you reckon I could make the *Sun*, Sam?" I had always wanted to appear opposite the inside front cover. And it wouldn't be the first time there'd been three tits on Page Three.

"Just wait and see, Rich." With that, the conversation ended, and it went straight out of my mind.

Fridays are always fish and chips day. It's the law. At every job I've ever had, from when I worked for the council to when I worked at a builders' merchants, the employees have eaten this British culinary delight religiously, and I see it as my duty to continue the Friday tradition even when I'm not working full-time. The Friday following my newspaper appearance was no exception, and I picked up my usual cod and chips and curry sauce on the way home from my part-time job. No sooner had I parked my car and raised the handbrake than my mother hurriedly rushed out to greet me.

"Thank God you're home. The phone's been manic," she said, clutching various scraps of paper on which she had kept the messages. "You'd better eat your dinner quickly. Some are about to call back."

"OK, I'll answer a few calls, stick my dinner in the microwave quickly, and then eat," I assured her as the phone rang again.

John Brown of the *Independent* was the first of many calls I took that afternoon on my home phone. My mobile was similarly busy. I managed a couple of forkfuls of fish after the first few calls before the phone rang again.

It turned out that my college lecturers, Jacqui Boddington and Mark Benattar, had also been taking calls for me at college all morning. They had rung my mobile several times (but I was ignoring it by now, trying to keep up with the landline). They finally reached me at home to tell me they'd received four calls from radio stations and to warn me that they had passed on my number.

My lunch was fed to the dog.

By five o'clock that evening, I had spoken to reporters from six or so national newspapers and had organised telephone interviews with several radio stations. It seemed everyone wanted a piece of me, and although I am nearly six foot five, I wasn't sure if there was a sufficient amount of me to go around. Somehow my short and seemingly innocuous article had spawned a circus. Frankly, I was a little overwhelmed. And still the calls kept coming. The media were like vultures (nice vultures, the kind that would arrive on time for dinner and not leave the corpse waiting before picking away at the rotten flesh) and wouldn't leave me alone until they were satisfied with the gatherings of their swoop.

As a result of the press coverage, I appeared in the Saturday editions of the *Guardian,* the *Daily Mail*, the *Sun*, the *Telegraph,* and the *Times,* and also was featured in the *Cornwall Independent* and the *Western Morning News* the following day. On Friday and Saturday alone, I did live interviews on BBC Radio Five Live, BBC Radio Cornwall, BBC Radio West Midlands, BBC Radio Cambridgeshire, and BBC Radio Wales, and had the privilege of talking to the BBC World Service from one of the Radio Cornwall studios that had kindly unlocked late on Saturday night especially for me. The curious appetite of today's media was summed up perfectly by the BBC World Service interview, as I received almost twice as much airtime as the story that aired just before mine, on the Rwandan genocide. There's something definitely disconcerting about that.

The other thing that niggled me about the newspaper and radio coverage was their constant comparison of Bateman and me to Butch Cassidy and the Sundance Kid, Thelma and Louise, or, most alarmingly, Bonnie and Clyde. Let's consider their endings. Butch and Sundance go out all guns a-blazing and die. Thelma and Louise get concerned and decide to end it all at the bottom of a cliff. The police took no chances with Bonnie and Clyde, choosing to unload 167 rounds of ammunition into the couple's car—50 entering the fugitives' bodies alone. No, thank you.

In the week that followed, I featured in Taiwan's *Taipei Times,* India's the *Hindu,* and *Reader's Digest*—at least the last of these meant I could reminisce about my American adventure whilst waiting for a doctor's appointment in six years' time. After further radio interviews with Manchester's Key 103, Beat 102/103 and RTE in Ireland, and Australia's 6PR in Perth and 720 ABC, I knew it was only a matter of time before the Americans found out about me and my illicit intentions.

It occurred to me that our relatively innocent holiday had already received more exposure than I would have liked. So much for the fun of spontaneity. I started to feel the crushing weight of people's expectations. If I wasn't careful, I would lose all control over the entire affair. Plus, I started to fear that if the Americans got wind of this, they might not let us into the country.

At least two productive things had come from the barrage of phone calls and articles, however: I had managed to memorise my mobile phone number (something I had never learnt before due to lack of calling myself), and I could boast a claim to fame that equalled the time I shook hands with Pope John Paul II.*

My fears about American law enforcement catching on to my plan were realised on March 3, when I received my first call from across the pond. It was an American who had read one of the dozen stories that had somehow made their way onto the stateside newsstands.

"Hi," he started cheerfully enough. "My name's Dave O'Brien, and I co-host the *Wank and O'Brien Show* in—" (I must point out to the American reader here that in the UK, the word *wank* is the most common slang term for masturbation. Simply, it's our version of your *jerking off.*)

"Pardon?" I interjected quickly. (Good job I didn't say "come again?")

Dave repeated his introduction and, after assuring me that his co-host's name wasn't at all comical in the States, requested an interview with me.

I agreed to the interview, which was to be taped for broadcast on their breakfast show the following morning. They invited me to join them live in the studio if I passed through

---

*In case you were wondering, I have indeed shaken hands with the Pope. During a school trip to Italy and Austria in 1994, when I was thirteen, we were taken to Rome to explore the Colosseum and Vatican City. It just so happened that on the day of our visit, the pontiff, who travelled in a bullet-proof automobile not dissimilar to a golf buggy, was blessing the crowd who had assembled in St. Peter's Square. Caught up in the herd, I decided I would copy what everyone else was doing and hold my hands aloft—it seemed the perfect time (and place) to put the saying "when in Rome" into practice.

Even at thirteen I towered above others, and when John Paul passed, it was my hand that he shook. My hand. Probably the only non–Roman Catholic hand within the entire Vatican.

There is now talk of John Paul becoming only the fourth Pope in history to be made a saint. Another claim to fame may be mine. I've shaken hands with a saint. How many people do you know who have achieved that? And in case you were wondering, Ian St. John of Saint and Greavsie does not count, nor does anyone affiliated with Southampton Football Club.

Indianapolis during my trip, and I was only too happy to agree. No way would I pass up the opportunity to sit opposite a man named Ed Wank. Once more, I was looking forward to the trip.

The calls and e-mails continued for a month or two following the news hype and it wasn't until my birthday on March 20 that not one single call or e-mail intruded, and I felt as if the whole ballyhoo had finally died down. I could return to simply looking forward to being a felon in the United States and planning the route we'd be taking.

Not fully trusting the Internet, I decided I would invest in a little more research to make sure the laws I was about to break were in fact real. I soon came across a book entitled *The World's Stupidest Laws,* written by a former Salisbury magistrate by the name of David Crombie. Many of the laws that I saw on DumbLaws.com didn't feature in the book, but a great deal of the funnier ones certainly did. I decided that I would treat the book as my Bible. If the law appeared within the pages of the book, I considered it a law. If it didn't, I didn't. Simple as that.

A road map, blank map outlines of America, and the book of laws sat on my living room table, and I was eager to break open a pack of fluorescent highlighting pens that I'd bought several years ago but never used. West to east had always been my preferred route, but now, with the extensive media coverage I had received in the States, I was seriously considering flying to Vancouver and crossing a land border where, I hoped, no probing questions would be asked before making my way down to San Francisco.

A few hours and a couple bottles of wine later, I had come up with an ingenious and foolproof plan. Across the road map I had plotted a series of numbers, each of which corresponded to the specific town and law in question. I could now calculate, almost to the hour, exactly when and where each lawbreaking incident would take place. It was very impressive, if I say so myself. A little too impressive, in fact, and when I finally realised that I had created a ridiculously strict itinerary that left no room for chance encounters or lost weekends, it wasn't long before, instead of taking its place on the wall, the plan was torn up and shoved in the bin.

"We'll just fly to San Francisco and take it from there," I told Bateman the next day.

The wave of media attention I received turned out to be a great blessing in hindsight. It definitely made me more savvy. Even the dreaded work experience had taught me something: six hundred words can get you in a lot of trouble. If I hadn't been prepared for a trip of this magnitude before, I certainly was now. No God-fearing southern-state sheriff would stand in my way. No cell could contain me and my date with destiny. If I could survive a three-month media barrage, I could handle eight weeks in an enclosed space with Bateman. I was ready for America, and in my eyes, July couldn't come quickly enough.

3

NOT THE START TO THE AMERICAN DREAM

Due to its position in San Francisco Bay, Alcatraz Island dominates any view from the many piers that make up Fisherman's Wharf, the most northerly point of the peninsula on which San Francisco sits. Before the rocky islet became the world's most feared high-security prison, the island was home to nothing more than the odd pelican (*alcatraz* in Spanish). From 1934, for almost thirty years, the island was home to some of the most ruthless criminals in America, the likes of Al Capone and Machine Gun Kelly.

The conditions were inhumane: darkened cells no bigger than 5 by 9 feet, and all inmates were kept in solitary confinement. The prisoners weren't allowed to talk to each other, play cards, or even read newspapers. Visits were heavily restricted to two hours a month. Nowadays, the only people on Alcatraz are tourists, and the queue that forms at Pier 41 every day shows just how much the stringent visiting regulations have changed. The island welcomes more than 750,000 visitors every year, all of whom are free to leave.

By taking a tour of the bay, the dreaded history of Alcatraz can easily be forgotten when one sees the sun break through the clouds, illuminating the island's lighthouse as the rays find gaps in the orange towers and suspension lines of the Golden Gate Bridge, which sits alongside as a constant bay-side companion.

Or so I was told.

As I stood on the wharf, the fog that plagues this part of California was so thick I could barely make out the rock on which Alcatraz stands. And as for the Golden Gate Bridge, well, my map assured me it was there somewhere. As I turned to face the city, the conditions were only ever so slightly overcast, and nothing except for the 853-foot Transamerica Pyramid building had sufficient height to penetrate the cloud cover. The difference in views was similar to the turning of a postcard.

Although we had no actual law to break on Alcatraz itself, I thought it an appropriate place to begin an American crime spree. But given the weather conditions, I could see the trip would not be worthwhile. Bateman and I had to make do with the shores of Fisherman's Wharf and hope it was at least the scene of some of the inmates' final steps on mainland soil, maybe even the scene of a scuff-up, to shine just a little light of infamy on the starting point of our felonious adventure.

We retreated to the hotel to regroup.

According to an old city ordinance that apparently has yet to be repealed, the country's most liberal city still forbids oral sex—given or received. At home, to meet a young lady and attain that level of intimacy given just one night would be nigh impossible due to my dull personality and undesirable looks. But in America, my track record, in that respect, was actually pretty good.

When I'd visited Los Angeles in 2002 for my twenty-first

birthday, my friend Chris and I decided to take a taxi to Hollywood after finding the name of a suitable strip bar in the daily newspaper. We figured that in any club with a name like Perversion, the night's proceedings were guaranteed to please. After arriving slightly early, Chris and I propped ourselves up at the bar to begin an evening of drinking. After a staggering number of vodka and Cokes at a pace that greatly concerned the barman, we looked around to see if anything had begun. The dance floor that surrounded the catwalk was beginning to fill with people, but no scantily dressed women had yet graced the raised platform with their presence. As Chris ordered another couple of drinks—using his credit card to pay for them, as we'd now run out of cash—I paid a visit to the toilets, meandering through the many people who had started to gather. As I passed each person, rubbing shoulders with many, I felt something just wasn't quite right, but I couldn't put my finger on it. I decided it would come to me eventually, and entered the toilet. After taking care of the necessary business, I turned to notice that a gentleman was offering me a towel to save me the complicated procedure of taking one myself.

"Thanks," I'd remarked as I took the towel and stared down at the man's selection of sweets, chewing gum, colognes, and other beautification products.

"You're brave, aren't you?" he'd replied.

"Pardon?"

"Dressed like that."

"Why, what's wrong with it?"

"Nothing. But every Thursday night is goth night. Didn't you notice everyone else?"

I opened the door slightly and peered back towards the dance floor. Everyone in the building had a white face, sported spiky black hair, and wore a long, dark trench coat. I must have been drunker than I thought not to have noticed that earlier. At least on the way back to the bar, Chris was easy to spot: he was the only guy in the club dressed like me in jeans and a shirt. We must have stuck out like clowns at a funeral.

"Um, Chris, I'm not sure if you've noticed, but tonight is goth night, mate. Just take a look around you."

Chris spun around on his chair and surveyed the scene before nodding slowly in agreement and turning to the barman. "Two more vodka and Cokes, please, mate."

Regardless of how we were dressed, we did manage to attract a few admirers who either took pity on our foolishness or found two club "rebels" intriguing.

Whilst I stood among a plethora of goth smokers, neither dressed the same as them nor with a cigarette in my hand, my English accent and pronunciation of the word *actually* made one particular girl weak at the knees. During the course of the evening, I used the word whenever I possibly could, and after one of the strangest evenings of my life, I would up paying for a taxi for us to her apartment before returning to my hotel the following morning. With the memories of that night fresh in my mind, I realised that my accent was my secret weapon whilst in the States. It was a trick I was only too happy to pull out of my sleeve in San Francisco.

The first evening of our lawbreaking trip began like any night in Britain would for Bateman and me. We drank eight or ten cans of Budweiser to warm up. Once we'd successfully taken care of that, we found ourselves walking back down towards Fisherman's Wharf as I wondered what other words might sound rather spiffing in a well-spoken English accent.

We found a suitable bar near the piers. The evening

continued like many of my nights back home—a couple more beers for Dutch courage whilst I studied the dance floor for a suitable target. Just then, Bateman spotted two unaccompanied young ladies at the bar. We made our way over to them, strategically positioning ourselves on two of the adjacent seats. Almost immediately two men returned and continued a conversation they had probably begun with the girls seconds before they had vacated the seats Bateman and I now occupied. I ordered another drink whilst Bateman went outside for a cigarette.

After ten or fifteen minutes of propping up the bar and drinking by myself, making doubly sure that only the odd one or two people were wearing black trench coats, I began wondering where on earth Bateman had gone. I ventured outside onto the club's deck to investigate. Happily ensconced at the top of the stairway, which many of the club's patrons had turned into a smoking hot spot, stood Bateman and two girls. The girls were quite attractive too. This was just what the doctor had ordered. Two American girls would get the spree off to a fantastic start in more ways than one. Just as I approached the girls to introduce myself with the line "*Actually,* you can call me Rich," or maybe a simple but effective "Actually, actually, actually," I made the shocking discovery that the "Americans" Bateman had cornered were in fact Swedish. I wasn't sure whether to feel sad or delighted. I was disappointed that my accent probably wouldn't work on them—but on the other hand, they were Swedish.

"Ah, you must be the lawbreaking guy," remarked Swede One deductively (I can't remember their names—shame on me).

"That's me," I replied, hoping Bateman hadn't let the cat completely out of the bag. "So, what brings you to San Francisco?"

"Oh, I was an au pair a few years ago and I'm just visiting the family I au paired for."

"What's an au pair?" Bateman quickly interjected.

"Remember that Louise girl who was accused of killing that American baby by shaking it a few years back?" I said. Bateman nodded. "That's what they do."

Bateman laughed. The Swedes didn't.

"I'm sure you didn't do *that,* though," I said quickly.

Good start, Rich. Maybe I should have gone with "actually, actually, actually" after all.

Back inside, we escorted them onto the dance floor and instantly gained their admiration when Bateman demanded the DJ play the song the girls had requested earlier in the evening—"Dancing Queen" by Abba. As the voices of Anni-Frid, Agnetha, and the rest of the Swedish group faded out, I was surprised to notice that Swedes One and Two had both remained with us. They stayed well after their song had been replaced by all manner of musical styles from hip hop and rap to dance. After a bit, Swede One was comparing muscles with Bateman, who had stripped down to his vest (or "wifebeater"). The fact that Swede One had sunk to Bateman's level and pulled the sleeve of her shirt up past her shoulder to show off her muscle had me smiling and Swede Two staring in disgust. As I noticed Swede Two's look of disapproval, I immediately changed my facial expression in order to curry favour with her. She was looking better with every pint. Just when things really started to look up, even without one "actually" leaving my lips, the girls informed us they had a plane to catch in the morning. With that, they left us with a brief parting kiss. Minutes later the house lights lit up the dance floor and the music ceased. There was no time even to find a desperate American girl to take home. I had failed. I had only given myself that evening in which to break a law in San Francisco before leaving the next day, and now it was over. And no, Bateman was definitely not an option—I wasn't that desperate.

The next morning, the hangover pounding through my head outweighed the bitter feeling of defeat. I knew that the first law was a difficult one, so I wasn't too disappointed by my failure. But I was eager to get at least one broken law under my belt. To achieve that, I would have to leave San Francisco. And for that, I needed a car. Without one, the whole crime spree would have to centre on my sordid activities following nightclub ventures, breaking the same San Francisco ordinance over and over again. Actually, maybe that wasn't so bad.

Budget was the closest, indeed only, car rental company within easy walking distance from our hotel, and after learning our lesson the day before on how ascending Everest-like hills in San Francisco pulling suitcases was a bad idea, we didn't feel the need to venture further afield. At the Budget office an elderly gentleman called Si greeted us. He offered us a car for $800, which seemed like a fair price. I already had visions of me at the helm of a blue convertible cruising down the West Coast, the refreshing northerly wind in my hair, two gorgeous female hitchhikers in the backseat, and Bateman in the boot.

That was until Si realised neither of us was twenty-five. This proved to be a big insurance problem, the effect of which was to raise the overall price by about a million percent. We left downhearted and empty-handed.

After several failed attempts to hire a car ourselves using the pay phone outside our motel and a page we had unceremoniously torn out of the hotel room's yellow pages, I did what any hardened criminal would do in this situation—I rang my mother at one o'clock in the morning her time.

After she had secured us a car using the Internet from her home (making her a fully fledged aider and abetter), Bateman and I found ourselves back at the airport to pick up the car, a 2005 Chrysler Sebring. It would be ours for the next three weeks until we reached Chicago, where, per the rental agreement, a new car would have to be hired for the jaunt to New York. The Sebring was brand-new and had almost no miles on the clock. We would soon take care of that. We headed south on Route 1 towards Los Angeles. We were officially on the road (albeit the wrong side), heading into the unknown in what I supposed would become our version of a getaway car.

Just twenty minutes out of San Francisco, the cool bayside temperatures had given way to the exhausting heat of inland California. The air-conditioning soon became a necessity, but all in all, driving in America was far from cool. Much of this could be attributed to the automatic transmission. Simply put, it removes all the pleasure, instinct, and skill from driving. Back in the UK, I'd have changed gears weeks ago, but here we were at the mercy of the engine's whims, regardless of our pleas, cries, demands, and eventual yells of frustration at the dashboard. Cruise control was handy, but when added to the already dull sensation of driving without a gearstick, it generated an experience behind the wheel that bordered on mind-numbingly mundane. In order to stave off extraordinary boredom, we began a highly competitive U.S. version of our favourite motorway travel game—Spot the Roadkill. (Basically, a player is awarded points if he or she spots a dead animal on or by the side of a main road. The rarity of an animal will decide how many points a player is rewarded for the find. For instance, a kangaroo would be worth next to nothing if an Australian spies a dead one in the outback, whereas if the same carcass was seen whilst circling London on the M25, then his opponent had better hope he sees a polar bear or dodo lying around in order to win. It's also a good game to keep the children quiet on long holiday drives and will dramatically cut back on the times you'll hear "Are we nearly there yet?")

We headed back towards the coast in search of the Pacific Coast Highway, turning off the interstate and consulting a map to see the best way of cutting through the Santa Lucia Mountain Range, which separated us from the sea. We didn't choose very wisely. Every "town" our road passed through seemed to be populated solely by farm animals. The mountains surrounding us were bare, desolate rock faces, where not even beasts dared to tread. Eventually, after several wrong turns we met another human being, who was happy to direct us to the coast. Unfortunately, he was a member of the U.S. Army, and the road he suggested to the coast passed through a militarised area belonging to the Fort Hunter Liggett Military Resort. We were free to travel on only after he had seen my licence and rental agreement. Luckily, he didn't enquire as to why we were in the country. Our every brake and steer was probably being monitored back in the barracks as we passed a forecourt where no fewer than twenty tanks and other military vehicles stood. One false move and we could be subjected to America's trademark "friendly fire." The road meandered on and on before finally climbing through the mountains. At the top, temperatures reached over 100 degrees. The Pacific was supposedly directly in front of me— pity the fog had travelled with us and I could see only a cloud-filled valley. To make matters worse, Bateman led the roadkill game a rabbit to nil.

After four hours on the road, exactly halfway between San Francisco and Los Angeles, we arrived in a tidy Morro Bay motel. The evening drew darker and the sun descended into the Pacific to the west. After the hectic first few days of flights, car worries, and lawbreaking failure, it felt good to relax and be at total ease with the surroundings. Palm trees stood just feet from our motel door, the Pacific rolled gallantly onto the shores just beyond, and a man nearby shouted profanities and vicious threats to the residents of the house opposite our motel.

From what I could make out from the bathroom, where I could hear his voice the most clearly, he was obviously drunk. He had some very harsh words to say to Chico, Charlie, and two other names I couldn't make out. Stepping out onto the balcony with a slice of pizza in hand to see if I could grasp a better understanding of the situation, I heard he wanted to slice their throats. I quickly returned to the bathroom, where I'd be safe from becoming his next target. After thirty of the most entertaining minutes I have ever spent in a bathroom, the police arrived and took the man away, ruining any chance of an encore presentation.

Baldwin Park, a suburb of Los Angeles, was my next target. In Baldwin Park it is illegal to ride a bike in a swimming pool. That seemed like a very rock-and-roll kind of law to break. After leaving Morro Bay, we first stopped to visit Hearst Castle, which stands on the hills overlooking San Simeon and the Pacific. U.S. publisher William Randolph Hearst's immaculate 90,000-square-foot castle, which Hearst called a "ranch," wasn't constructed until the media mogul was in his forties. His parents forbade it while they were alive, saying he would "go too far." They were wise. In 1919, just two months after the death of his mother, Hearst, on whom the famous film *Citizen Kane* is based, and architect Julia Morgan stood on the empty hills and made his parents' nightmare come true. They broke ground on a home with fifty-six bathrooms, sixty-one bedrooms, and its own cinema. As Bateman and I stepped onto the bus that winds the seven miles up the mountains from the coast, I naturally jumped onto the five seats that stretched across the back, just as if I was embarking on a school trip. The duration of the drive is timed perfectly to match a prerecorded talk on the history of the castle. They cater to Europeans rather too well, and every time they mention a unit of weight, size, distance, or height, they follow with a conversion. The constant translation of pounds into kilos, miles into kilometres, and feet into metres made the tape last twice as long as necessary. When we finally made it to the gates of the castle I felt I would never require the use of a conversion table again.

Bill, our guide, welcomed us as we stepped off the bus and marched up to the top of the castle's granite steps. He talked us through the rules of the visit—"keep within the velvet ropes," "don't lose the rest of the group," etc.

"And kids, if you're thinking of throwing a coin into the fountain and making a wish, I guarantee you there's more chance of that wish coming true if you keep hold of your money."

As Bill cracked the same jokes he's probably been making for the entire twenty-six years he's been a Hearst Castle guide, I began to feel less like an aspiring criminal and more like a camera-wielding tourist. This could have been due to the fact that I was in a foreign country and carrying a camera. I wanted to feel infamous, not one of the crowd. I hung back, as did one other tourist, an Israeli bloke, both of us a bit embarrassed by the over-the-top enthusiasm of the American contingent of our group. We Brits pride ourselves on our reserve. The constant and completely unnecessary choruses of "wow," "gee whiz," and even "you'd better believe it" that followed one of Bill's facts really grated on my nerves. One lady asked if the living room furniture had been there when Hearst resided was in residence—despite the fact that Bill had already explained twice to us that nothing had been altered; a girl was told off numerous times for touching the marble and leaning on several household items; and I can't remember the number of times a camera flash went off, even though we'd been informed at the beginning of the tour that it was strictly forbidden. At this point the only thing I wanted to do was to return to the bus and learn how many acres make up a hectare. It was even making Bill pretty twitchy. Just when I thought that the tour couldn't end quickly enough, we entered the final room, which turned out to be my favourite.

Hearst's Roman pool, styled similarly to the baths of Caracalla in ancient Rome, is magnificent and typifies the whole palatial complex. The walls, covered in mosaic tiled patterns inspired by Italian mausoleums, together with the eight marble statues of Greek and Roman gods that surround the pool, exude a profound air of significant affluence and astronomic extravagance. The roof, adorned with stars and other galactic entities, replicates a truly out-of-this-world experience. We were told that the tiles lining the pool and covering the walls from ceiling to floor are each an inch square, were all placed individually, and required half of the builders' seven-year construction time to complete. As refined and English as I was, even I had to contain an unnecessary whooping noise after that statistic.

The timing of our arrival in Los Angeles after we finished the tour wasn't great. L.A. produces the kind of traffic jams where reaching speeds in excess of 20 mph makes you feel as if you have broken the sound barrier. Not even the twelve-lane highways that cater to L.A.'s thousands of commuters are large enough to cope with the traffic's demands. Rush hour is at its peak at five. We arrived at five on the dot. It took us two or three hours to travel just twenty-five miles east of the city and towards Baldwin Park.

Breaking law number two sounded simple, but I suspected it could prove quite a challenge. I was confident that hiring a bike would not be a problem, but I needed to enlist a motel proprietor who would understand what I was trying to do, and allow me to do it.

I would never get the chance. Who would have foreseen that the suburb of Baldwin Park had only a public swimming pool? Out of the three shabby motels we found there, not a single one of them had a pool. Using the public swimming pool would have definitely qualified, but I felt it would be very difficult to smuggle a bike through the showers towards poolside. We eventually stayed in a motel in the neighbouring suburb of El Monte, only a mile from Baldwin Park. The accommodation was far better than what we had seen in Baldwin Park, and we had full use of all of the motel's amenities: cable TV, fridge, iron and ironing board, and, ironically, a swimming pool.

I was bitterly disappointed. I had been in America for only four days and already I had been defeated by the two laws I had attempted to break. I knew neither failure was due to any fault of my own. My parents were to blame for my looks, and I couldn't ride a bike in a pool that didn't exist. But in my mind, bottom line, I was a failure. My frustration had reached boiling point, and I simply needed to break a law to stop the run of bad luck we were having, even if it wasn't as exciting as riding a bike in a pool or receiving oral sex. Suddenly inspiration struck. I instantly ran to the shop opposite the motel to check out the fruit and veg section.

California law states that you are prohibited from peeling oranges in a hotel room. Returning to the room, I displayed a blatant disregard for the law by spitting in the face of authority and peeling not one orange but three.

That'll show 'em.

4
CALIFORNIAN CRIME WAVE

I hated Los Angeles. It was a seemingly endless expanse of urban sprawl. But there was still one law that I wanted to tackle in California before we moved on to a new state. In the afternoon, when the temperature fell back into the seventies, I would bravely curse on a mini-golf course in Long Beach. I'd heard a lot about American miniature golf courses, and from what I'd seen in films and on TV I know they were anything but miniature. I was expecting giant clown heads and twenty-foot windmills where to get the ball safely on the green, you'd have to send the ball between the blades as they rotated. To be honest, anything would have been an improvement on the British version of the game, where the toughest shot choice you'll encounter is deciding which side of the building brick to aim.

Before making our way to Long Beach, Bateman and I decided to visit some of L.A.'s famous surfing spots—hoping that this might salvage some kind of Los Angeles beauty in my eyes and give us a better impression of the place.

Although Huntington is technically a suburb of Los Angeles, it's far enough away from the noise, crowds, and multitude of interstates and byways that you can actually get out of your car and enjoy the town, its pier, and its people, whose only rush seems to be in the direction of the water. Since surfing first hit the mainstream with help from films such as *Endless Summer* (1966), Huntington Beach with its prominent and unmistakable pier has become a California mecca for surfers. The day of our arrival was no exception. Even though it was just an arbitrary Wednesday morning, when you'd think people should be either at work or running errands and chores, the sea was peppered with body boarders, surfers, and the ubiquitous and obligatory long boarders (the perennial vision of "old school" and "natural" surfing). Behind us, still more boarders crossed the road with their boards under their arm, hurriedly passing people who had donned their sandals and slung a towel over their shoulder to simply enjoy the beach. We soon remembered that the American summer holidays had begun two weeks before we had arrived, and this accounted for the weekday crowds. From the pier, children could be seen playing volleyball on one of the many courts that lined the beachside footpath, or simply enjoying the beach and the remainder of their twelve weeks in the sun. Lucky sods.

After our brief pit stop in Huntington, Newport was next on the list, only about twenty miles further down the coast. I needed to find an Internet café to e-mail the children at the primary school where I used to work. I had promised to keep the class up to date on my American adventures and to respond if they e-mailed me. Not wishing to corrupt young minds, I mentioned nothing of the true nature for my visit to the States.

With a population of over seventy thousand, Newport Beach had evolved from a simple surfing hot spot. Its surprisingly large downtown area, with several high-rise buildings, was proof of the city's prosperity, so I thought I'd have no problem whatsoever finding somewhere from which to send the e-mail. We followed the signs that directed us to tourist information. From there we were directed to the nearby mall, where they told us to go to the library. I couldn't believe I hadn't thought of the library before. An Internet café, bar the muffins.

I quickly typed the e-mail to Mr. Rice's class, attached a few pictures, and openly invited questions from the children. Most of the e-mail was about my visit to the Hearst mansion and the weather—well, you have to, don't you? Leaving the library, Bateman and I visited the Newport Wedge, a famous shore dump (where the waves break directly onto the banks of the shore and rarely into deep water) that can reach in excess of 20 feet. Today the sea was like a mill pond, and a couple who passed me on a tandem seemed more threatening.

It was soon time to leave. The drive to Long Beach would take us back through Huntington via the many towns that straddled the coastal road. Bateman was driving—theoretically so I could make notes on our travels to date, but really so I could sightsee. I expected to regularly pass petrol stations and fast-food chains, but for every mile we drove, I saw more and more palm readers and psychics plying their trade and using bigger and better signs to attract potential customers who either feel little self-assurance or are just plain gullible. Back home I wouldn't have the faintest clue of where to go to visit a psychic, but here I was being offered palm readings and visions of my future at almost every set of traffic lights. After passing the fifth one in as many minutes, psychic peer pressure got to me, and I reasoned that due to the uncertainty of my future in the States, I ought to pay one a visit. I decided to do so as soon as we reached Long Beach.

Before we got there, we had to navigate an American roundabout (or traffic circle), which had made its first appearance. After not having taken a single picture with my camera in San Francisco, I quickly put it to use to capture our first encounter with a traffic circle on film.

Now, I know what you're thinking—what's so special about a roundabout? If you're English, nothing much; if you're an Englishman in America, a great deal. I once travelled around America with my dad, and in five weeks we had driven more than 11,000 miles. In all of that travel, we came across one single roundabout (incidentally it was the Long Beach one, and we were so shocked by its sudden approach that we took the wrong turning). One appearance in all that distance makes whatever roundabout you do see something very unique indeed.

Just up the road from the splendour of the roundabout I spotted a psychic's sign. You couldn't miss it—it was thirty feet high. I was expecting a Madame Enigma or something similar, but the gargantuan sign in her front garden informed me that my future would be seen by Brenda—a rather bland name for a psychic. Brenda operated her business from her home in a rather prosperous area of Long Beach, and apart from the massive sign, the house seemed pretty normal, with a cupboard for sale for $40 on the front lawn. Tentatively I climbed the steps to the front door and tapped nervously on the insect-proof wire door frame.

The door opened to reveal a woman in her early fifties, with tied-back ginger hair. She clutched the doorknob in one hand and a bowl of stir-fry in the other. She stared vacantly at me as if I was a door-to-door salesman.

"Hi, are you . . . um . . . open?" I asked, not really sure of the term for a currently operating psychic.

"Yes, I am. Come in," she replied, changing her mood completely. Now she was upbeat and ready to go, like a schoolkid who had been kept in class for ten extra minutes and had finally been released into the playground and wanted to make up for lost time.

Bateman and I sat in her porch, which seemed to also function as her consulting room. She disappeared into the house for a moment. The porch was cosy and split into halves. The left-hand side, from where Bateman observed, was dotted with Buddhist statues and randomly placed Irish memorabilia from Guinness posters to shamrocks and leprechauns. I sat in the Jesus half, where his image was everywhere. Dozens of porcelain statues, shelves of postcards, and framed pictures of the Messiah dominated my side of the porch. The single appearance of a style-his-hair troll (remember those from the nineties?) and the compulsory crystal ball were the only non-Christian items in sight.

Just as I was about to begin an impersonation of a palm reader, Brenda emerged from the house and positioned herself opposite me. Sitting this close to her, I could clearly see two boils—not on her nose, like you'd expect on a witch or psychic, but situated between her neck and chest.

"What do you want? Tarot cards, palm reading, or your future read?" she asked.

"I'll have the cheapest, please." And anything that didn't involve looking into her crystal boils.

"If you want to know how your trip in the States will go, it'll be the future reading," she replied. Of course that was the most expensive. "To read your fortune, I will need something that is yours and has only belonged to you," she instructed. The only things I had on me were my clothes, which I planned on keeping, and money, which I was sure someone had previously owned.

"How about a flip-flop?" I asked, thinking on (and about) my feet. I proffered one in her direction.

"No, that won't do!" she said strictly.

What was wrong with a flip-flop? As far as I was concerned, she was going to make my future up anyway.

"I haven't stepped in anything," I said.

"How about your sunglasses?" she asked, pointing at the collar of my shirt, from which they hung.

I had completely forgotten they were there, and gave them to Brenda. She held them in both hands and pulled them close to her chest. Too close to the boils for my liking.

"Yes, you are a strong man, you like to be independent, and you were born to be successful."

"OK," I replied, knowing full well that was probably the usual spiel she used to put her clients at ease.

"By the end of the year I can see a change of location for you."

"I was planning on moving house by the end of the year, actually," I said. My scepticism was still strong, but Brenda was beginning to crack me.

"You will be happy with a girl, but there will come a time when you must decide between two."

"Two? That many?" I replied with a smile. I was beginning to enjoy my fortune. Then Brenda's permanent smile turned upside down.

"Don't get into a red car," she warned, making serious eye contact.

"Pardon?"

"Someone will offer you a lift in a red car during your stay here. Don't get in. Danger," she reiterated.

"Thank God our hire car is blue," I joked. But Brenda was far from laughing.

"Beware of a white-, silver-, or blond-haired man. He cannot be trusted financially."

"OK . . . although that does only leave me with black- or ginger-haired people. Anything else?" I inquired.

There was silence for a moment. "I see, I see . . . a court case."

"Great, just what I need."

"Someone will take what you're doing seriously and you

will appear in court." I had told her why I was in America, and so that wasn't as surprisingly accurate a premonition as it sounds.

"Can I have some nice stuff again?" I asked.

"You will invent something and make money out of it."

I stared blankly back at Brenda with my bottom lip protruding.

"Do you know what it is?" she asked.

"Nope," I replied conclusively.

"Are you sure?"

Even if I did know, I wasn't about to tell her. She'd steal my idea. And, more to the fact, I didn't have one. "No, I seriously don't know."

Maybe some fresh premonition was racing through the lens of my sunglasses and through to Brenda's senses, or else she was bitter that I wouldn't give away my idea, as she instantly changed the subject for the worse.

"In the next eight weeks, someone will confront you and you must walk away." I stared at Bateman and pointed straight at him.

"Oh, no. I'm sure it won't be your friend," she said.

"It probably will be, you know," he said, sitting back in his chair, as if he'd already had that premonition himself.

"Yeah, and I'm a coward and always walk away anyway. I even run sometimes," I added.

Brenda made several more startling revelations about me owning my own business, and then asked me if I had any questions about my future.

"Only one," I replied. "Is there a mini-golf course in Long Beach?"

"No," she replied.

"Shit. Are you sure?" My scepticism in psychics reached an all-time high.

"I'm positive. My husband and I used to play a lot of

mini-golf, and the course in Long Beach closed two years after we were married. What must it have been now? Probably 1971."

"So I'm a tad late, then? Are you absolutely positive that there isn't one within the Long Beach city limits? Not even by the *Queen Mary*? Loads of tourists go there."

"You can use the Net and look if you want."

So even psychics use the Internet. I was invited into her home to use the computer and found that the closest miniature golf course to Long Beach was in a town called Wilmington, only two miles away.

As I left her house, I turned to Brenda and asked the question I'd really wanted to ask from the moment she first opened the door. I'd originally thought it to be rude, but now I blamed Brenda for the third failure of our holiday, and so it was time to ask.

"If you're such a good psychic, why don't you just display the cupboard on the lawn on the day you know someone who will buy it is going to walk by?"

That told her.

Back in the car. I needed some cheering up, and Bateman was certainly not equipped for the job.

"So much for the spree, Rich," he said. "You may as well just write a detailed account on the roadkill we find. At least we've had a lot of success there."

"Hey, things'll pick up," I replied, trying to convince myself. "It's just not the best of starts. That's all."

Before we could leave Los Angeles, Bateman, a habitual gym visitor back home, insisted we go see Venice Beach and the famous Muscle Beach gym. We had to buy an Arnold Schwarzenegger "Governator" T-shirt. Bateman, after an endless perusal of the merchandise, finally selected a "My

Governor Can Kick Your Governor's Ass" T-shirt, and we were set to nab a bite to eat and leave.

Only two blocks from the Santa Monica pier, you'll find a branch of the restaurant chain called Hooters. The bright white and orange colour scheme makes you think of the old diner days of America in the fifties, but inside, the show is anything but a reminder of more conservative times. Their motto provides a clue as to what we would expect from our meal: "Men: No Shirt, No Service. Women: No Shirt, Free Food."

A stunningly attractive girl who, like all the other waitresses, was dressed in nothing more than a white vest and very tiny orange skin-hugging shorts showed Bateman and me to our seats. I went for the Hooters Burger, which had so many ingredients, it sounded more like an obscure German musical instrument. Just as our food arrived, "YMCA" by the Village People came blasting out of the speaker system, and floor service went on hold as all the waitresses climbed on whatever furniture happened to be in their vicinity to dance upon. Two teenagers and their grandmother sat at the table next to ours, and when the dancing began, I looked across, expecting to see the reaction of a shocked pensioner. To my surprise, the boys tried to pretend they found the bubbles in their fizzy drinks more entertaining than the free show, while their grandmother applauded and cheered for every shoulder shake and bottom wiggle.

I was reenergised after lunch, and it was time for Bateman and me to join an endless queue of traffic and take the crammed six-lane highway slowly out of the city and head east in the hope the spree would improve.

At 6 p.m., after almost three hours, the gridlocked Los Angeles traffic finally gave way to open lanes. This was probably due to the fact that we were now more than thirty miles outside downtown, already drawing near to Palm Springs, a city that stands alone amidst towering desert mountains. The evening temperature was still unbearably hot, and so we took a dip in the motel's swimming pool. It did nothing to cool me down. The day's heat, which had remained at a constant 110 degrees, had warmed the small pool up to the point where my "cool-down" swim was far hotter than I usually have my bath.

Next morning we paid a visit to the nearby library in Cathedral City to check our e-mail. The Riverside County Library Service was now the third American library of which I was a member. As expected, the e-mail reply from the children lay in my inbox, and I opened it, wondering what kind of questions they were going to ask. Only one of the children, an impish boy called Joel, knew why I was really here. I had met him at a cricket match shortly before I left and told him everything. The rest of his class thought I was simply in America for a holiday.

Joel must have said something.

"How are you going to get a giraffe?" wrote Kane and Damon. "Do you know where the cheese factory you're going to fall asleep in is?"

Christopher added salt to my slowly healing wounds by asking: "Have you found a bike and a swimming pool yet?"

The questions that followed were closer to what I'd been expecting. Chantelle, Emily, and Hayley enquired as to how cold it was at the top of the mountain where I had taken the pictures, and the rest of the girls affectionately stated that they missed me and wanted me to come back—before bizarrely asking me if I'd seen a baby koala. Joel (who clearly cannot be trusted with a secret), Luke, and Samuel addressed more pressing, grown-up matters and asked: "How are the chicks?" But it was Ben and Jake who asked the most important question of the lot: "When are you going to stop being silly?" I've yet to get back to them on that one.

Indian Wells, California, statute number 9.04.020 (Musical Instruments—Use in attracting customers for sales) decrees: "It is declared to be a nuisance and it is unlawful for any person vending, advertising or soliciting the sale of, or assisting in vending, advertising or soliciting the sale of any kind of notions, merchandise or medicines in the City to use a musical instrument or device, or to sing or call out or to make any noise to attract persons for the purpose of vending, advertising or soliciting the sale of notions, medicines or merchandise."

In other words, you may not play a musical instrument with the intention of luring someone into a shop. Easy. In order to get this crime spree back on track, I had to do just that. I headed to Toys "R" Us for the tools I'd require. I thought I'd try a trumpet. Having never played a trumpet before, I didn't know what I should look for as far as quality. Lucky for me, only one model was on offer.

For a mere $8.99 I purchased what I can only describe as a three-in-one electronic trombone, trumpet, and saxophone (because that was what was written on the toy's packaging). Indian Wells was, more or less, exactly what I expected, and it appeared to be the same as the towns we'd passed through to get there—towns like Rancho Mirage and Palm Desert, whose names offer a pretty accurate description of the places.

After taking the batteries out of my digital camera and placing them into the instrument, it was time to find an ideal place to put my snake-charmer-like tones into practice. A nearby arcade of stores seemed like a nice spot in which to play, and a position outside an antiques shop and opposite a supermarket was selected. Several people passed and stared at me strangely as I played, but not a single one decided to enter the shop. They didn't need to. The law stated I had to have the intention to actually lure them in, and as I began to direct their attention by raising my eyebrows and tilting my head in the direction of the doors, it was clear what my overall aim was. After several minutes, no customers, and slightly sore fingers, I removed the trumpet from my lips, took a bow, and pressed one of the sound effect buttons on the side of the toy, which produced rapturous applause, congratulating myself on a law well broken. It was just a pity there was no one there to see it.

5

The "Welcome to Arizona—The Grand Canyon State" sign was truly a welcome sight for me. My expectations after putting the disappointment of California behind me were as high as the temperature, which by now had reached a stupidly high 120 degrees. Back home, people complain when temperatures spill into the 90s. The searing desert heat meant we could leave the car only if absolutely necessary and the air conditioner had to work overtime.

Unlike California, Arizona had only one law for me to break, and our destination was the small town of Globe, 230 miles east of the border, where it's illegal to play cards against a Native American. Our illegal activity in Indian Wells had resulted in a later-than-anticipated start, so we decided to spend a night in Phoenix.

We checked into a hotel south of the city. I sat in the lobby making use of their free Internet access, and it wasn't long until Jennifer, the desk clerk, began to talk to me, seemingly about anything that came into her head.

"So you guys spell *tyre* with a *y*, huh? How strange."

The constant interruptions resulted in one e-mail taking more than an hour to write, but along the way I managed to consume four cans of lager, teach Jennifer all about the British Empire, and come to understand why the Tower of London guards had got annoyed with Jennifer and her friends on her recent visit to the capital.

Bateman returned from using the hotel's gym and joined me in the lobby with his own can of lager. For a Friday night, the hotel was very quiet, and drinking seemed the only activity worth pursuing. It wasn't long until we were joined by Joye, a delightfully amiable woman who lived north of Phoenix in Flagstaff and was visiting her Honduran-born mother, who worked in the hotel. During the ensuing conversation I discovered Joye used to live in Globe, and I enquired as to what I should expect from the town and, more importantly, how difficult it would be to find a Native American.

"You shouldn't have too much of a problem finding an Indian in Globe," Joye explained encouragingly. "Any bar'll have quite a few, I reckon."

After declining several offers, Joye finally accepted one of our cans and endearingly referred to it as a "pint." We appreciated an American making the effort. "I'll only have one," she explained. "I have to be up early tomorrow."

It didn't take long, probably due to Jennifer's perpetual presence behind the desk, before the conversation turned to America's education system, as I have only ever heard bad things about it. I expected Joye and Jennifer to defend their country's teaching, but Joye was definitely not sluggish in her response. "It's terrible. Especially here in Arizona."

"I've heard that some high school graduates can't even point to America on an unmarked globe and naturally point to Russia because they assume it's the biggest. Is that true?" I asked.

"I wouldn't be surprised. They aren't the brightest," Joye

replied. Jennifer didn't agree with Joye's pessimistic assessment of the U.S. education system but was caught short when asked where Beijing was. She was surprised by the answer. "Is it? Well, I thought it wasn't in America."

The beer had run out, and as Bateman left in search of an outside drinking establishment, I bid farewell to Joye and retired to my room.

Next morning I awoke fully clothed and realised I was up early enough to make use of the hotel's breakfast service. The dining room was practically empty, so I sat down next to the only other occupied table—beside what appeared to be the only other guests in the hotel, who turned out to be Joye and her mother.

"Mom, this is Richard. He's one of the cleverest guys I've met. He's the one going around America to break all the silly laws," said Joye as my struggle to open a cereal packet proved Joye's kind introduction to be very much inaccurate.

"Hi. Very pleased to meet you. Joye tells me you're originally from Honduras," I replied as I greeted her with one hand whilst forcefully ripping the packet of Lucky Charms open with the other and scattering the cereal everywhere.

Since an early age, I've always retained strange facts about countries and have often taken pride in recalling them, although to this day they have proved to be nothing more than useless information that resists any attempt to remove it from my brain. By now I must possess a fact for most countries in the Western world. I can only hope this knowledge holds me in good stead if ever I want to sound intelligent whilst in the presence of a foreign national.

For some reason I know Canada has more land water than the rest of the world put together and that Tajikistan is the home of the world's tallest dam. I can hum the Qatari national anthem. Honduras' fact was easy to recall because it's a double-whammy and can be used for two countries.

"Were you in the country when Honduras had a six-day war with El Salvador over a World Cup qualifying match?" I asked excitedly (it was one of my favourite facts).

"Oh. Yes. It was terrible; there was panic in the streets. Riots and rapes were frequent, and my parents hated each other. You see, one was Nicaraguan and the other Honduran."

"Oh," I muttered.

Perhaps in the future I should stick with the fact that Honduras is the third-largest garment supplier to the United States.

After I said my goodbyes to Joye and her mother, it was time to hit the road once more to travel the ninety-two miles east to Globe. Route 60, a far cry from the interstates to which Bateman and I were now accustomed, made its way sinuously through rugged, bleak, and inhospitable cactus-ridden landscapes. The road passed through many unremarkable and easily forgettable towns, and it seemed no time at all until we made our final turn through the Superstition Mountains and saw the town of Globe ahead of us.

You'd be easily forgiven for thinking Globe's population was much greater than the official figure of a little over 7,000, due to the number of motels that greet your arrival. And it seems every fast-food brand is represented. Burger King, McDonald's, Domino's Pizza, and Taco Bell all vie for customers on a stretch of road where a stable and blacksmith's shop would seem more appropriate.

We decided to combat the heat with a quick swim in our motel's swimming pool, which was conveniently located outside our door. After the quick dip amidst the uninvited leaves and discarded crisp packets, we returned to our room to discuss our strategy for the night's lawbreaking. Just then, the weather took a decided turn for the worse.

The small white clouds that hung in the sky as we drove into town had vanished, replaced by what was now a menacing grey sheet. As I began to dry myself off, the sky became darker and released a cacophonic crash of thunder. The heavens opened. In a matter of seconds, the torrential rainfall had turned the flower bed outside our door into a pool of murky water, and the winds had picked up to a terrifying speed. I slammed the door firmly shut and we watched the storm from the comfort of our room. I felt glad about the timing of our swim and how lucky we'd been not to be in at the start of the storm.

"Back in the pool!" Bateman shouted at the top of his lungs.

"What?" Sometimes I marvel at his stupidity.

"In the spa. It'll be warm in there, it'll be great," he replied with a certain degree of persuasive logic. Well, enough to send us back out into the storm and into the spa.

Soon we were happily ensconced in the jet-streamed warm waters of the spa, the storm still howling and wailing around us with increasing ferocity. The rainfall that pounded into my cheeks and eyes felt as hard as pellets of hail. The buildings on the other side of the road had by now become invisible behind a curtain of unremitting rain, and the empty chip packets with which we had previously shared the pool had been easily swept away. As the winds increased, Bateman and I were reduced to shouting at each other in an attempt to communicate amid the crashes of thunder and fork lightning that illuminated the dull and dismal sky, wondering if it was now a better plan to return to the safety of our room. Our decision was cemented when an umbrella suddenly caught the wind and rushed toward me at a terrorising speed in what seemed to be a direct course, as if it were possessed. At the last second, the umbrella wedged itself into the steps used to enter the pool—directly in front of where I was sitting.

We raced back to our room, and as quickly as it had arrived, the storm lost strength, the clouds parted, allowing the sun to once again beat down upon the town, and Globe was exactly as it had been when we had arrived an hour before. Albeit a bit soggier.

By now it was early evening, and although the temperatures were still in the low 90s, it was time to leave the motel and make our way down to the historic downtown area to find bars, shops, and—we hoped—Native Americans. As we left, we waved to the motel manager, who was still trying to fish the pool furniture out of the deep end.

Downtown Globe was a ghost town. Well, in fact, quite a few people milled about, but it was just how I pictured an old cowboy town to be: a single, dusty road with buildings hugging the streets and more or less nothing of any interest at either end. As Bateman and I strolled up the main street, it seems as if it could still be used as a setting for a John Wayne or Clint Eastwood movie. Not even the neon "open" signs and the rows of pickup trucks parked diagonally to the sidewalk were enough to break my reverie of times of lawlessness and showdowns at high noon. At the side of the road, a plaque dedicated to the law enforcement of Gila County commemorates the "hanging tree" from which L. V. Grime and C. B. Hawley were lynched on August 24, 1882 for the holdup murder of three men. A shop awning had been brought down during the storm, and the proprietors were examining the damage; across the road the local cinema had been gutted in a fire the week before. The town's historic air had got the better of me. My overactive imagination decided that the awning had actually fallen in a shoot-out with culprits who were eventually flushed out of their cinema hideout by the sheriff's order to blitz the building.

Back to the task in hand. We needed to find a Native American, and on Joye's earlier recommendation, Bateman and I peered through restaurant and bar windows in order to find one. Early inspections proved unsuccessful, but we put that down to the fact that it was still only five o'clock on a Saturday evening.

The most popular bar in town seemed to be the Drift Inn Saloon, with tables outside. Since the finer points of the law decreed that cards were not to be played *on the street* with a Native American, this bar seemed the obvious choice of watering hole. But the building's eerie likeness to Wild West drinking establishments made entering the saloon seem a daunting prospect. The moment we did, all of my earlier cowboy dreams came flooding back.

The Inn had been founded in 1902, and judging by the lack of air-conditioning and layout of the bar, it seemed only the clientele and brands of drinks had changed since then. Tables stood empty, and the fifteen or so stools at the bar provided adequately for the evening's patrons. Men in white vests and baseball caps sat alongside butch-looking women with tattoos. A Hispanic lady was serving behind the bar, and two young men traded shots on the pool table. Not one of them looked Native American. We took two empty chairs at the bar and ordered a couple of bottles of Bud. I was quietly hoping that an Indian would simply walk into the bar, but after the disappointing start in California, I was determined to see this one through, no matter how much effort it took. After fifteen minutes of waiting, Bateman and I moved over to the pool table to pass more time and to gain a superb vantage point on the rest of the bar. After a couple of games,

I became aware of two men paying close attention. One was a pug-nosed man who sat at the end of the bar and watched our games intently, as if he had a wager on the outcome. The other was a younger guy dressed in a T-shirt and ripped jeans who was playing the table next to ours.

"Who just won that game?" asked the young man as he approached to shake my hand.

"Um . . . he did," replied Bateman, pointing his cue at me.

"You want a match?"

As I broke, the young man chalked his cue and took his opening shot. "We'll play your pool rules, shall we? English rules."

"In that case, that was a foul," I replied. "You didn't even hit a ball."

As the game progressed, I noticed that he was either purposely playing badly in a very poor hustling attempt or was simply very drunk. I won the game quite easily and waited to refuse his request for a rematch—this time for money. It never came. Drunk.

"So, what're you doing in Arizona?" he asked as we both placed our cues back in the rack, which definitely confirmed there was to be no rematch.

"I'm here looking for a Native American, really. You don't happen to know any, do you?" I asked hopefully.

He looked right into my eyes. "You can't turn back the hands of time, man."

"Right," I said, not knowing what on earth that was supposed to mean. He staggered back to his friend. I took that as a no, then.

We returned to the bar. By now an hour had elapsed, with no Native American encounters and just a pool victory over a drunkard under my belt. As we ordered our next drink, I asked the bartender if Indians often drank there. Her answer appeared to be a wild guess but was more than encouraging: "Yeah, we're expecting one any minute now."

"Any minute now" turned to ten "any minutes now" and then to twenty. I grew impatient as the temperature began to drop and with it, the sun's position in the sky. Just as I thought about changing bars and maybe having to resign myself to another night in Globe, a man walked up the steps to the bar and entered. I only got a quick glimpse of him as he strode past me before perching himself on an empty seat at the opposite end of the bar, but his jet black moustache and rough, tanned skin made me feel that my search might be at an end. I quickly stood up and examined him further. The suspect was dressed casually and certainly didn't stand out from the bar's regulars: jeans, white T-shirt, and the mandatory baseball cap. I tried to picture him in Indian regalia, complete with ceremonial headdress. The bottle of lager in his hand could well have been a tomahawk.

"That's our man!" I said to Bateman. "Let's go sit by him. There are two empty seats at his side of the bar."

We positioned ourselves alongside him. Bateman looked on expectantly as I took a few minutes to compose myself and prepare my gambit.

What do you say? You don't just ask someone to play cards with you because you think they're an Indian. I thought of offering to buy him a drink, but he seemed to have had two already and might get the completely wrong idea about my intentions. Just then he turned, creating my opening.

"Hiya. You couldn't do me a big favour, could you?" I offered my hand for him to shake. "My name's Richard Smith and I'm over here from England breaking silly laws in America. In Globe it's illegal to play cards against a Native American in the street, and I was wondering if you could have a quick game with me. It'll take just two minutes of your time."

Remarkably, this didn't faze him at all. The man took the drink away from his lips, laughed, and shook my hand. "Why, sure. It should be fun."

The Native American's name was Arden Deloris, and as we took our seats outside, the light was beginning to fade. A moderate breeze blew down the street, probably a remnant of the earlier storm. I produced a pack of cards from my shorts pocket as Arden opened his wallet in order to show me something.

"This proves how Native American I am," he said, handing me the green card. It gave the name of his tribe: Laguna Pueblo. "You see, I speak like a white man and look like a Mexican, but I'm full-blooded Indian," he added. "So, what game do you want to play?"

"What games do you know?" I replied.

"Shall we play king's corner?"

"I've never heard of that game. Do you know how to play rummy or poker?"

"No."

So it turned out that finding a Native American was the easy bit. I should have remembered that between them, any two people know the rules to nearly every card game there is, but very rarely do they share the knowledge of a single one.

"How about Snap? I'll teach you the rules to that. It's simple," I suggested. It took me less than a minute to teach him, and a little under a minute after that I had half of the pack, Arden had the other, the game had begun, and the law had been broken. Almost instantly two sixes appeared, and Arden looked at me as if he wasn't sure what to do.

"Snap!" I said, slamming my hand down on the table and

claiming the cards. This blatant act of unsportsmanlike play only injected fire and competition into Arden, who won every hand from that point on, easily beating me at my own game. I never was good at Snap.

"So why is it illegal, then?" Arden asked, much later than I'd thought he would.

"I don't know, but in South Dakota three Native Americans walking down the road can be considered a war party and may be fired upon, so you should count yourself lucky that you're only banned from playing cards here," I replied, bringing a smile to Arden's face. Bateman, who had been taking photos of the epic Snap battle, had now joined us at the table, and soon we were both engrossed in Arden's tales of his life and his people. For the first time on the trip so far, we sat and listened to a stranger, not interrupting or cracking jokes, but just drinking in every word.

We only did play that one game of Snap, but remained outside well after the sun eventually went down. Over a few drinks, it transpired Arden would remain in Globe for the next two years as a heavy machinery worker in the construction industry. The name of his tribe, the Laguna Pueblo, is derived from two sources—the Pueblo are his people, and they reside in Laguna, New Mexico. It's an eight-hundred-mile round trip from Globe, one that Arden makes every weekend to see his family. He is a proud man who knows his skills are highly regarded by his employer but takes greater pride in his son, an eighteen-year-old who is currently at college in Denver (studying to work in construction like his father). Feeling sentimental, Arden unclipped his mobile phone from his belt and left a loving message from father to son.

When I asked Arden if he thought working in construction and so far away from his tribe made him feel if he was losing his Native heritage, he shook his head.

"I'm one of the few people in my tribe who can still speak the language. I'll teach my son the same way I was taught, and I'm hoping he will do the same," he remarked solemnly.

By now it was getting dark, and as Arden made his way back inside, Bateman and I moved in the opposite direction to the car. As much as I'd enjoyed drinking and talking to Arden, we had reserved the late night for a trip to the Indian reservation casino 10 miles out of town.

With the lawbreaking back on track, having broken two in a row, Bateman and I thought it best if we hired a taxi to take us to and from the casino so we could both drink to celebrate and lose money at the same time.

"Could we get a taxi to the casino at quarter past eight, please?" asked Bateman, on the phone with a nearby taxi company that had been suggested to us by the motel manager. "No. A quarter past eight . . . No. Eight-fifteen, not eight-thirty. A *quarter past* eight."

Whoever was at the other end of the line obviously had a problem with telling the time, so instead of asking the man to arrive at our hotel when the big hand had reached the three, Bateman settled for eight o'clock.

Our phone rang at eight on the dot, and we made our way to the lobby, where a small man stood clutching a set of keys.

"You wanna go to the casino?"

Now, I can't say I was expecting a yellow cab or a stretch limo to be waiting for us, but I imagined there'd at least be a taxi sign or plaque of authentication stuck to the rear of the vehicle. This car had neither. The blue 1989 Mercury Grand Marquis, which would never have passed its MOT in England (a test that ensures the road safety of a vehicle) and had no indications or markings to reveal it was a taxi, but we were assured it was by the man's wife, who sat at ease in the passenger seat.

"Let's hope it doesn't rain. This baby doesn't do so well in the wet," she remarked. Bateman and I simply stared at each other across the roof of the car and entered regardless.

As I sat down in the back on the driver's side I squeezed in between workmen's helmets, which were digging into my back, and a selection of coats and other garments on the floor, making it impossible for me to put my feet anywhere but to the side. It was humid and stuffy inside, and I would have asked our driver to open his window to aerate the car if the glass had not been replaced by a strip of cardboard fastened to the rest of the car by masking tape.

Other than the uncomfortable seating and worrying condition of the "taxi," the ride could not have been more pleasant, and I began chatting to our driver. As it turned out, our chauffeur and wife used to sell medical supplies; now, out of work and with trailer park rent to pay, they rented their car out as a taxi. After trying to explain several times that not all Englishmen live in London and in fact we lived more than three hundred miles from the capital, the wife handed Bateman a flyer.

"Here's our number when you wanna get picked up later on," she remarked. "Don't worry about how late it is."

The piece of paper she handed to Bateman had "NEED A RiDE GlobE MiAMi CLAyPooL" crudely written above their telephone number in black Biro. For some reason, a picture of a tricycle pulling a trailer provided the centrepiece.

"Um . . . thanks," replied Bateman, folding up the flyer and placing it into his back pocket.

The car eventually pulled up outside the front doors of the casino, and as I tipped the driver handsomely for delivering us safely and not stealing my kidneys, he announced to the door staff in a loud, strong tone: "Take care of these guys. They're from London!"

After taking two hours to find and play cards against one Native American, we were about to spend the entire evening on a blackjack table in competition with a dozen of them.

6
CALL ME RICHY

Flagstaff lies a mere 90 miles from the Grand Canyon's southern rim and seemed the perfect place to stay overnight after leaving Globe the previous day. Utah, where the next law awaited me, was well within striking distance, and as the canyon blocked our path no matter which way we decided to get there, it seemed ridiculous to simply bypass the opportunity to visit one of the seven natural wonders of the world.

It was nine-thirty on a Monday morning when we left our Flagstaff motel and arrived in the centre of town, where the laid-back, northern Arizona attitude had a dramatic effect on rush-hour traffic. As we walked from the library through the main park and into the downtown area, the roads were almost devoid of vehicles, and the constant honking of car horns with which we were now familiar had been silenced. Sidewalks were lined with more trees than people, and the panoramic view of the snowcapped mountains that surrounded the town together with the refreshing 70-degree temperatures made the entire experience an extremely pleasant one. We strolled over the train track that bisects the town just in time to hear the signal that sounds to welcome the famous Santa Fe Railroad to town. As we watched the barriers fall, the few cars that were left to wait did so patiently as no fewer than sixty-five carriages were pulled at a sauntering pace by six forbidding diesel engines. As the train passed and slowly made its steady ascent into the mountains, I turned to Bateman to remark on how beautiful the town was and that it was easily my favourite thus far. Bateman's reply was quick and decisively blunt. "It's rubbish—there's nothing here."

Time for the canyon, I thought.

It's not easy to describe the Grand Canyon. Everyone has seen pictures and knows it's a giant chasm carved into the rocks of the Colorado Plateau like an open wound in the side of the earth. The awe-inspiring view of the prodigious canyon that took thousands of years to form and is now well into its umpteenth millennium of creation shows its true beauty when, with the exception of the click of tourists' cameras, there is silence. In a country where grandeur and magnificence are flaunted and held aloft for all to see, the canyon sits in perfect serenity and peace, safe in the knowledge that its simple existence is its greatest appeal.

We quickly got back into the car and drove to a further number of viewing points along the southern rim of the canyon, finishing at Mather Point and Desert View, where the open plains of northern Arizona and southern Utah can be viewed beyond the precipices of the canyon. It was here that I experienced an acute sense of boredom, as if I'd seen it all before: all viewing points, however spectacular, are very similar in a way. Admittedly, I was ashamed to feel this way and was chastened to acknowledge that it is very difficult for me to remain in awe of something, even on a scale of this magnitude, for a prolonged amount of time.

As we were leaving I noticed a word on the map that I had

learnt only a few days previously: Pueblo, both the name of Arden's tribe and the name given to a specific type of Indian village in the American Southwest. It just so happens that one of the Grand Canyon National Park's points of interest are the ruins of the Tusayan pueblo. It seemed a perfect opportunity to learn some more about local native cultures.

The ruins were nothing special, and it took less than a quarter of an hour to walk past the two-foot-high remnants of five or so buildings that were first built there over 800 years ago. The nearby single-room museum's walls, adorned with traditional puebloan attire, weapons the tribesmen may have used, and artistic perceptions of what the settlement might have looked like hundreds of years ago, are overshadowed by the view the inhabitants would have had. Instead of the steep descents of the canyon's ridges and desert plains, the settlement stands in perfect view of Humphreys Peak, Arizona's highest point, 46 miles south of the canyon and home to a community of Hopi—a tribe comprised of Tusayan descendents.

As we left the Grand Canyon, passing a myriad of Indian stalls selling all manner of things, my attentions turned to the road map to get us off the troublesome mountain roads and back onto the interstate, where travel was boring but speedy. We crossed the border and into Utah, where Route 9 seemed the easiest—indeed only—way back to the interstate. It was with some degree of confusion and bewilderment that we found ourselves in Zion National Park, where we were asked to pay a $20 entrance fee. Even though we only wanted to use the road to get back to the interstate, it seemed the fee had to be paid. As we entered the park, Bateman wasn't at all pleased.

"Twenty bucks! There was a sign back there that said 'Don't feed the animals.' I'm gonna run them over, get my money's worth, and watch them scrape it up. Bastards." (Of course, extra points are awarded if the roadkill is caused by the player.)

I had arranged to stay with my friend Lee James in Salt Lake City because the next law was relevant throughout the entire state of Utah, and by now I thought nothing of driving an extra 200 miles to see a friend. Unfortunately, the scenery remained mountainous but bland, the lack of roadkill did nothing to ease the boredom, and the appearance of a light-house in Cedar City, more than 400 miles from the coast, proved the only thing of any interest during the three-hour drive.

We arrived in Salt Lake City a little after three in the afternoon and parked outside Salt Lake Motorsports, where Lee worked. Lee, an eighteen-year-old who'd moved from Cornwall to Salt Lake City with his dad and stepmum almost three years before, wasn't expecting me so early, and as I shook his hand, I couldn't contain my shock at how he spoke.

"My God, you even speak like a Yank!" I shouted in the middle of the shop. "How long did that take to change?"

"Well, I *have* been here almost three years," Lee replied, probably thinking he'd made a terrible mistake in inviting me to stay. Lee, who now says *gas* instead of *petrol* and *couch* instead of *settee* but is vehemently proud he pronounces *garage* the English way, informed us that he knew of at least two roundabouts near where he lived, and he promised to show me when he finished work at six. Until then Bateman and I would have to amuse ourselves. With no other tourist attraction to speak of, we headed for the Great Salt Lake.

The Saltair, a mosque-style building with dome-capped

minarets, is a redundant shadow of its former self. Before the turn of the twentieth century, the building was built by Mormons to provide a "wholesome place of recreation," and at its height in the 1920s it attracted nearly half a million visitors a year. The attraction, which once was at the water's edge, now stands in a dilapidated state in front of an empty car park, more than half a mile away from the water due to years of drought. The inside contains a single shop, leaving the rest of the building empty. The dance floor, once the biggest in the world, leads the way to grand spiral steps that arrive at an abandoned mezzanine level. The building was the third to be built on this site, after its predecessors were both lost to fire. Outside, two rusty train carriages have been left to corrode in the salty environment and are the only memory of times when they ran throughout the day to cope with the visitors' demand. We walked towards the water's edge across the seemingly solid sand, which when stepped upon cracked like old glass, and were met by a dead fish lying just yards from the shore. Nothing seemed to survive here. The lake, which from the shore appears as wide as any ocean, has a lingering smell of sulphur and, with the exception of hundreds of thousands of flies that cling to the remaining dry sands of the beach, is lifeless and still.

A couple of hours passed quickly, and we made our way back to Salt Lake Motorsports in time to see Lee and a work colleague wheeling the mopeds from outside the front door into the shop. Lee was also accompanied by an attractive girl with long black hair and perfectly straight white teeth, whom he introduced as his girlfriend, Jen. We followed them in our car to their home in Tooele, a twenty-minute drive away (thirty if you take a detour to show an Englishman an American roundabout).

"I got a caution from the police because I left skid marks

in the top of this roundabout," he said proudly. "You want me to show you the other?"

"No, mate. I've had enough roundabout excitement for one day. Save it for tomorrow."

From the first gas station after leaving the interstate from Salt Lake City to Tooele, we purchased a crate of lager for the evening; after discovering that Utah law caps alcohol content at 3.2 percent, we bought another.

Lee is the proud owner of a black Trans Am (almost identical to the one used in *Knight Rider*—minus the red fairy lights at the front) and before we decided to crack the crates open, he took us for a quick Trans Am experience. A quick wheel spin that filled the air with a distinct smell of rubber, acceleration up a road behind his apartment, and a handbrake skid later, Bateman and I found ourselves back outside Lee's apartment and wanting a Trans Am ourselves.

Sitting on their balcony whilst making short work of the lager, I produced the book of laws and proceeded to explain, once again, how I was intending to spend my summer.

"So, how are you going to hunt for a whale in landlocked Utah?" asked Lee.

"Simple—I'm going to hire a boat at a lake somewhere and as long as I'm at least trying to hunt the whale, surely the law has been broken," I replied.

We drank into the evening, and I tried to steer the conversation away from my crime spree so I could be more of a friend and not only talk about myself. I turned to face Jen.

"So, have you lived here all your life, then, Jen?" I asked.

She shook her head. "I was born in Georgia. Then my mom and I moved to Montana because she met a guy there. Then his grandparents died and we inherited their house in Iowa, so we moved there. Then my mom died, so I moved to Florida to be with my aunt before moving back to Montana to be with my grandma. Then back to Florida to be with a guy who ended up going to Japan with the navy, but my aunt, who I was staying with, turned psychotic, so I moved to Kentucky to be with my dad, but his wife and I don't get on, so I moved to Utah, where I met Lee and we got a place together."

"Oh. That's a no, then."

We continued drinking on their balcony well after the sun went down and into the early hours of the morning. The absurdly low alcohol content resulted in eighteen empty cans of Budweiser resting at my feet alone, and shortly before two in the morning I decided it was time for bed. I had a whale to hunt the next day, and I left Bateman and Lee still talking as I made my way to the apartment's spare room. No sooner had my head hit the pillow than I was soothed to sleep by the sound of Lee throwing up in the bathroom opposite my room.

It had been four days since my illicit card game with Arden in Globe, and as I woke up, I was desperate to violate an ordinance that would bring my overall lawbreaking success record up to 50 percent. Bateman and I headed back towards Salt Lake City.

During the initial press coverage before I left home, I read a story written by a man called Matthew D. LaPlante, who worked for the *Salt Lake Tribune*. Unlike the others, LaPlante's report was not at all in favour of my plan and instead suggested I reconsider my criminal itinerary in Salt Lake City. Like a true spoilsport, he had contacted legal experts, who found no such law banning the hunting of whales in the state. However, later in the story, the state Division of Wildlife Resources spokesman Mark Hadley informed the reader that "the federal Marine Mammal Protection Act makes it illegal for any person residing in the United States to kill any marine mammal—anywhere." The last time I checked a map of the United States, Utah was still one of its fifty states, and therefore it was illegal to hunt marine mammals within its boundaries. Tenuous logic, maybe, but good enough for my purposes.

After finding a suitable nearby lake that had boats available for hire, I booked one for later on in the evening, by which time Lee and Jen would have finished work. In the meantime, Bateman and I had another day in which to prep the hardware. Wal-Mart was a stone's throw away from Lee's house in Tooele and seemed the perfect place to purchase the supplies—even if I had to construct a whale-hunting device myself. One of Lee's butter knives, a roll of duct tape, and a 98-cent broom with the head unceremoniously snapped off made an ideal spear. I was ready to hunt.

Our target, Jordanelle State Park, lies thirty miles east of Salt Lake City and contains Jordanelle Resevoir, where the hunt would take place. This was not so much because we thought we had a greater chance of finding the heavyweight mammal but because the Great Salt Lake smells funny and we didn't want to have to spend a day there. As we arrived and surveyed the beauty of the park, all seemed to approve the choice of lake . . . until they saw the choice of boats.

"What boat have you hired, Rich?" enquired Bateman. "It had better not be one of those pieces of shit there," he added, pointing disapprovingly at a row of four-seaters.

"Well, I went for the cheapest, so it probably is one of them," I replied, smirking at my own stinginess.

"You tight bastard!" yelled Bateman. "I'm not getting in that crap. I'm hiring a Jet Ski."

"You can't," I snapped. "We've passed their hiring times; I only got this because I asked really nicely for an extra half hour."

Bateman eventually acceded, and all four of us waited on the small wooden jetty for one of the "pieces of shit" to be driven around to us. We clambered in and were each handed a lifejacket retrieved from the murky brown water that had already made its way into our boat.

"You don't have to use it, but it's nice to have if you need to," remarked the assistant helpfully to Jen, who was already convinced we weren't coming out of this alive.

"Any chance of encountering some whales in the lake, is there?" I asked jokingly.

"Nah. Should see plenty of driftwood, though," he replied as he quickly talked me through the controls of the motor and rules of the lake. A "no wake" zone surrounded the jetty, which meant that speeds were to be kept to less than 5 mph until we were a safe distance away from the area. He showed me the choke, throttle, gears, and emergency stop, and as soon as he allowed us to leave, I forgot the lot, stalling the engine as I tried to pull away. My second attempt went more smoothly, but as our 13-horsepower engine propelled us painfully slowly away from the jetty I wondered why he'd bothered to inform me of the speed limit at all.

"You have to be the one to do it, you're American," I said to Jen, handing her the spear I had so beautifully prepared. "The law did say you had to reside in the U.S."

Jen took the weapon in one hand, raising the other to her forehead as she looked across the lake into the sun. She seemed as if she was taking it seriously, holding the spear and gritting her teeth whilst we took photos for posterity— she demanded several be taken in case her hair or posture wasn't to her liking.

"Let's go swimming," announced Lee, who had already taken his shirt off in preparation. Bateman agreed and also removed his shirt, sending the boat into a swaying frenzy as he launched himself into the lake's deep, clear water.

It was obvious I was never going to kill a whale in the lake, but the wording of the law meant Jen and I had to hunt for one, and that simply meant searching. With forty-five minutes of hire time remaining, I felt we had achieved this, and Lee took over at the motor. The lack of whales, and driftwood for that matter, must have had an effect on him, and he turned his attention to a crane that kept appearing around us, causing him to send the boat unexpectedly lurching in all kinds of directions in an attempt to run over it.

As we watched the sun drop below the pastoral hills that surrounded the lake, we pointed the boat in the direction of the jetty and headed back towards the land. We still had twenty minutes of hire time remaining, but with the speed of the engine we all agreed jokingly that it probably wasn't enough time to get back.

On the drive back to Tooele, Jen invited us to stay for another night, but her invitation was interrupted by an episode of the roadkill game.

"Moving roadkill," Bateman remarked observantly. "A deer." A pickup truck had overtaken us, and in the back lay the remains of a deer, resting as peacefully as if it were asleep.

"Surely that's a game winner?" asked Bateman hopefully.

"I don't know," I replied, wondering what the roadkill judging panel, if such a thing existed, would say. "Moving roadkill is bloody good, though." (We later decided a dinosaur would be considered "ultimate roadkill.")

"So, are you going to stay another night?" Jen repeated.

"Don't many people stay around yours, then?" I asked inquisitively.

"One of Lee's friends did once, but he tried to have sex with me."

"Oh."

"You gonna stay?"

How could we refuse? Motels weren't cheap, we were starting to get to know Salt Lake City like the back of our hands, and staying with Jen and Lee was a joy. As a result, Lee suggested we all hit the booze again that night and go to a club in town.

What a great idea, I thought. As far as the laws went, I was now four and three (as American sports fans say) and in need of a celebration. I might not have captured a whale in the lake that day, but I was definitely ready to party. And as Lee so nicely put it, it was time to "go out and do some proper whale hunting!"

7

The morning began with my fourth hangover of the trip so far and the disturbing revelation that Bateman was still only on his second pair of boxer shorts.

"Yeah, they'll do," he remarked as he held the garment to his nose, inhaling the aroma. "If not, I can always go back to using the first pair anyway."

The talk of underwear reminded me that I had a cheese factory to ring, and with Lee and Jen only owning mobile phones and both being at work, I headed to the Tooele library to make the all-important call from a landline.

Throughout the entire state of South Dakota, it is illegal for anyone to lie down and fall asleep in a cheese factory. Why it was against the law to do so, I wasn't entirely sure, but I could only assume a terrible accident had once occurred after someone had dozed off whilst inside. It was also one of the very first laws I chose to include on the trip, as it was as bizarre as the laws got. The problem I faced was that I had already sent numerous e-mails to the Valley Queen Cheese Factory in the small South Dakota town of Milbank. They hadn't replied to any of my requests to sleep in their factory, and even though I'd offered to work a shift as payment of the stay, they didn't seem to regard my communications with the sincerity with which they were sent. Throwing caution to the wind, and considering no news as good news, I rang them anyway.

"Good morning, Valley Queen. Which department?"

"Um . . . I'm not really sure. I'm ringing to request to stay in your cheese factory one night this week. Who would I have to speak to for that?"

"One moment, please, sir."

I waited as she patched me through to, most probably, the factory's resident psychiatrist. Eventually a genial-sounding lady spoke. "Mary speaking. How may I help you?"

I introduced myself, explained what I was doing, why I was doing it, and everything else that seemed pertinent before revealing the nature of my call. "I'm ringing you because apparently it's illegal in the entire state of South Dakota to lie down and fall asleep in a cheese factory, and I was wondering if there was any chance I could do so in your factory."

Mary sounded surprised. "Well, I've never heard of that law before, but due to state health and safety regulations, there is no way you would be able to spend the night here."

"Oh," I replied, heartbroken. One of my favourite laws, and I was shot down before I could even attempt it. "So there's no way at all?" I asked, injecting a sense of panic and desperation into my voice.

"No."

I was clutching at straws.

"How about if I just lie in the foyer with the security guard? That's in the factory, that'll count. He'll like me, I'm sure. We could tell each other all the things we've ever wanted to say but didn't have the time."

"I'm terribly sorry," she replied firmly, "but from the Valley Queen Cheese Factory, and probably every factory in the state of South Dakota, it's a no."

"Thanks anyway."

So that was it. Another failure had reared its ugly head just when things were starting to look up. Well, at least I didn't have to travel 400 unnecessary miles this time to experience it. I felt a sudden loss in energy and slumped into a chair by the phone opposite two girls who had heard the entire conversation and were probably wondering if it was safe to talk to me. They stood up, walked a couple of steps towards me, then disappeared into an aisle. I suppose they decided it wasn't in their best interest to begin a conversation. Alone in the Tooele public library and with a hangover from hell, caused in part by a girl who the night before insisted we buy drinks that came in test tubes, I found myself back at a 50 percent success rate once more.

I returned to Lee and Jen's and broke the news to Bateman. He didn't seem too bothered by the revelation, as he was still concerned about his boxer shorts dilemma, eventually playing it safe and remaining loyal to pair two.

The cheese factory was a bitter blow, but its failure presented us with an open path to Chicago, one that didn't have to pass through South Dakota. I consulted the map and my bible of laws, searching for something good in Nebraska, Kansas, Iowa, or Wyoming. Nothing. I couldn't believe it. I had the chance to change my entire route and visit four new states, but there was no kind of stupid law that I could break. In Nebraska I'd have to be a parent, a daughter, a barber, or a hotel owner to break any. In Marshalltown, Iowa, I'd have to transform into a horse and eat a fire hydrant (neither of which I was too keen on), and a law in Newcastle, Wyoming, decreed that it was illegal for couples to have sex whilst standing inside a store's walk-in meat freezer. Even if I could find a girl, I was sure that once inside the cramped conditions of a meat freezer, I wouldn't be able to warm to her. Kansas had the sole law that even tempted me, and only for a second. In Natoma it was illegal to practice throwing knives at men in striped suits. I've never thrown a knife in my life, and such is my hatred for pinstripes that I might not aim to miss. I looked closer at the map. If I couldn't find a replacement, the next law waiting to be broken lay in Chicago—almost 1,400 miles away.

Salt Lake City had become very familiar to us, and as we drove from Tooele back into the city to meet Lee for lunch, I enjoyed not having to consult a map or ask for directions. The downtown area was sparse and never gridlocked, and although many of the city streets were seven lanes of one-way traffic, the immaculately clean sidewalks and surrounding summer snow-topped mountains exuded a sense of freedom.

After joining Lee at the tail end of his lunch break, I explained to him that we were no longer in a hurry to leave, as we had plenty of time to make our way to Chicago and no criminal acts on the agenda. He asked if we wanted to stay for a further night, and on the condition that we didn't drink and condemn him to another hangover and that it was OK with Jen, we accepted. We left Lee to return to work as we tried to kill some more time and get ourselves a bite to eat.

A visit to the nearby Arby's restaurant meant we were slowly adding to our already impressive tally of fast-food joints visited. We thought it would be rude not to try each of the numerous outlets at least once, and Arby's, which specialises in roast beef sandwiches, now featured on the list. But what was of much more interest to me was what stood alongside the restaurant. Friday seemed a strange day to open

a store, but the sign suggested it was indeed the grand opening of Dollar Tree, and with my love for British pound shops,
I jumped at the chance to visit an American version. The
electric doors took what seemed like forever to open, and I
stepped inside, taking a deep breath. It smelt exactly like
they do in Britain—a musky smell of tattiness.

"Breathe it in, Bateman. Breathe it in."

The trouble with American shops is that their price tags
lie. Different states have a different amount of sales tax to
add to different products, and the tax is tallied up only once
you get to the checkout. In the United States, a child who
has a dollar in his pocket to buy sweets must add the total
up in his head and then add tax in order to work out
whether he has enough or has to put them back. Utah's sales
tax stands at 4.75 percent, making this a $1.05 shop, not a
dollar shop, as the sign suggested. This, however, didn't
matter to me. My mind was thinking of pounds and pence,
and I quickly had my brain working hard on the case. If this
was a $1.05 shop, then at the current exchange rate that
made it a 58-pence shop! My heart was pounding. If the telephone call earlier in the morning had been disheartening,
this experience definitely made up for it. Rows of deodor-
ants stood juxtaposed with packs of twenty scouring pads;
tasteless bags and handheld electric fans sat in baskets in
plentiful supply; and the toy section was full of blatantly
cheap replicas of well-known games with unimaginative
titles such as Mega 4-in-a-Row and Who's Who? It was
brilliant.

We had already bought Lee and Jen their weekly shop and
copious amounts of alcohol as payment for our stay, but the
invitation of one further night gave me the idea to buy them
presents. We decided we would get them matching frog and
tiger water wings (no particular reason), which they could
use that evening in the communal swimming pool they and

their fifty or so neighbours shared, together with one other present each. We split up in search of that special gift for our respective recipient (I was buying for Lee and Bateman for Jen) and reconvened at the checkout ten minutes later with presents in hand before finally leaving the shop. As the door swung open, it nearly hit a vending machine, which, I noticed, sold the *Salt Lake Tribune*. Wondering what Mr. LaPlante was moaning about this week, I quickly produced two quarters and bought a copy. We returned to the car and I began to flick through the pages, searching for his name. The national and local pages featured no article by him, nor did the sport, lifestyle, or any of the other sections of the paper. After reading a couple of uninteresting local stories, we ingeniously recycled the paper as wrapping paper for our gifts. The water wings proved deceptively tricky to wrap, but the 12-by-4-inch sock ironing board that I'd bought Lee was much simpler. Bateman, who had decided to use most of the remaining duct tape (left over from the construction of the spear) to adequately secure the presents, had an even easier time with a picture frame he had bought that depicted a couple having a wonderful time on a yacht—a gift we hoped Jen would hang on her wall as a fond reminder of our whale-hunting experience.

Back in Tooele, gifts unwrapped and graciously accepted by our hosts, we all went for a swim in the pool—unfortunately without the frog and tiger water wings. Upon our return to their apartment I explained the situation the cheese factory had left me in, with 1,400 miles to our next destination and no law to break. Jen took the book of laws, flicking straight to the Iowa page.

"What about this law?" she asked, pointing at an Iowa law that states it's illegal for any kiss to last longer than five minutes. "Why don't you break that one? I used to live there; I could get someone to do that."

"Could you?" I asked, sounding pathetically desperate. "I looked at the law but didn't really think twice about it. Easily doable?"

"Should be. Most of my friends are pregnant, though."

Jen explained she used to live in a small town called Fontanelle. *Fontanelle,* I remembered, was the word used for the soft spot on a baby's head. No wonder everyone there seemed to be pregnant.

The following day marked the beginning of our second week in America, and there was nothing to celebrate. Fontanelle was over a thousand miles away, Chicago even further, and after three enjoyable days in Salt Lake City, it was time to say our goodbyes to Lee and Jen. Packing our bags, I left the three-in-one electronic instrument as a final gift for our hosts, and we made our way for the last time from Tooele to the city. Lee's house can't be more than ten miles from Salt Lake City, but the fact that it stands on the other side of a colossal hill, reminiscent of the Scottish Highlands, almost doubles the distance you have to drive. Taking a wrong turn and heading toward a tiny set of houses, we passed a charming grocery shop that stood at one of the exits of a roundabout in the road. This must have been the second roundabout Lee had mentioned when we first arrived in Salt Lake City, and now I'd found it all by myself. Either that or Salt Lake City was the roundabout capital of America. Say whatever you want about the Mormons' religion—they make a bloody good traffic circle.

We finally got back on track and stopped to say goodbye to Lee at Salt Lake Motorsports. Bateman and I returned to the car and joined I-80, a road on which we would remain for the following week until our arrival in Chicago.

After only a few miles, traffic on the interstate dropped off and the road began to climb into the mountains. It's on the interstates in rural areas that driving in America really becomes a nuisance. The six lanes of the cities give way to just two, and a simple glance out of the window can be life-threatening, as taking your eyes off the road can result in hitting one of the shreds of truck tyres that litter the road in the hundreds. Overtaking is also a major problem. Cars' failure to pull over when we were behind them was getting Bateman annoyed, and the fact that they left their car in cruise control instead of slowing down made the entire operation a long, drawn-out affair that seemed like it took an eternity to complete. And there was little roadkill. New games we devised just didn't keep us enthralled. We did begin to count the number of carriages pulled by passing trains. A 75 was followed by a 68, then an 82, and finally a record-breaking 107. Like I said, though, this game wasn't enthralling, and little happened until we entered Wyoming.

"Roadkill!" shouted Bateman whilst chuckling to himself. "It was a bear! I'm sure of it," he added.

"Shut up," I snapped. "It couldn't have been a bear."

"It bloody was. It was massive."

"What kind of bear, then?"

"I dunno—it didn't have a head. It was a mysterious headless monster."

With no one around us, Bateman increased our speed to well above the 75 mph speed limit, a welcome way to get through the dull drive. Suddenly the flashing of lights and the wail of a state trooper's siren behind us gave us a highlight in an otherwise uneventful day. Not wanting to be struck by the fast-moving interstate traffic, the official made his way to my side of the vehicle.

"Do you know why I've stopped you, sir?" he asked Bateman after I'd wound down my window and generously greeted him.

"Maybe I was going a bit too fast," Bateman admitted.

"A bit fast? Ninety-seven in a seventy-five zone. I clocked you while I was driving the other way. Can you join me in my car, please?"

As Bateman acquiesced to the trooper's invitation, I used the car's rearview mirror to follow the action taking place in the squad car behind. The entire ticket writing seemed friendly enough: the state trooper sat and talked as if he'd known Bateman for years, and Bateman seemed at ease, hardly fazed by the double-barreled shotgun that sat alongside him.

"What happened?" I asked as Bateman returned to the car.

"Two-hundred-twenty-dollar fine." Bateman smirked proudly. "Gonna take that home and frame it. If I don't pay it, a warrant will be issued for my arrest in a month's time."

"You gonna pay it, then?" I asked.

"Bollocks I am. Two hundred twenty dollars! That guy said if I don't pay it, I won't be allowed to leave the country."

"He was bluffing, I reckon," I added helpfully.

"Yeah, that's what I reckon. And look, he spelt the name of my town wrong. I live in Redruth, not Redroof, like he's written. I reckon that's void."

"I don't think that voids the offence, Bateman."

"Don't care if it doesn't, I ain't paying it. It's just a good job he didn't clock me ten minutes ago. I was doing about a hundred twenty."

So the two-week anniversary was something to celebrate after all: Bateman had joined me in lawbreaking. Before today, he had been the official photographer at all the lawbreakings, but he had never actually broken one himself. He'd even passed up the opportunity to peel an orange in California. Now, after breaking only one law, he had superseded me. He'd been warned by a law enforcer and been threatened with arrest. Lucky bastard. In a month's time,

Bateman could be a fugitive, and I think he liked the thought of that.

Bateman had single-handedly brought the ratio of success to failure in terms of our lawbreaking endeavours back to five out of nine, restoring the successes' slender lead. As we made our way to our motel for the night, I-80 felt less like a long and tiresome road to Chicago and more like the road to recovery.

8

I woke to find myself fully dressed for the second time on the holiday, television still on and no Bateman. We had definitely both checked into the Oak Grove Inn in the Nebraskan town of Grand Island (which was neither grand nor an island—not even a peninsula), but now he had vanished and his bed appeared to have been slept in by the entire contents of his suitcase. I began to retrace our steps last night in my head to figure out where he could be, and took a walk to the lake that was situated at the foot of our room's patio door. The previous night had begun in the bar next to the motel, since we had arrived too late for a meal. That I could remember. I found a half-empty pizza box by the television on my return to the room—a major clue. The fact that it was a jalapeño pizza triggered the first of my memories of the evening and, although I lacked a deerstalker hat and magnifying glass, I was on the case.

We had left the pool table after I lost every game we played, returned to the bar, and started talking to a man about American sports. I'd commented how baseball was just rounders, American football shouldn't be called football at all, and basketball was the worst game ever invented.

Luckily for my face, he'd seemed to agree and we spent most of the evening talking about soccer, which I eventually convinced him was the real football. Then I'd ordered the pizzas, allowing one of the barmaids to choose one of the toppings. I hate jalapeños and would never have chosen them. Nor would Bateman, who I remembered hadn't ordered anything. He had left me in the bar and gone to the attached club, called Voodoo. I'd meant to join him, but for some reason, I returned in a merry state to the motel and watched the U.S. Open of Professional Eating. All the excitement of the spaghetti bolognese round must have sent me to sleep fully clothed. But the biggest piece of the jigsaw was still missing—where was Bateman?

Checkout time was eleven, and at ten forty-five, after a shower, I explained to the desk clerk that I would love to check out but couldn't owing to the fact that Bateman's room key was still in his possession. Thirty minutes passed, and after packing my suitcase into the car and perusing the *Grand Island Independent* provided in the foyer, I took a walk to the club to check that his body wasn't lying in a ditch somewhere outside the front doors. It wasn't.

As midday approached, all manner of scenarios as to what had happened to Bateman raced through my head from the simple to the absurd. I didn't think he'd take off with the travelling circus without telling me, and how on earth was I going to explain to his mother that a pack of hungry wolves had viciously butchered him on the 50-yard walk back to the motel? If Bateman was dead, I thought, he could at least have had the decency to wait until we had reached Georgia, where it's a crime to swear in front of a dead body whilst it is lying in a funeral home or coroner's office. I decided that he was most likely just waking up in his cell with a court appearance date looming. Everything fitted the story—he wouldn't have known the motel's number and therefore wouldn't have been able to use his one phone call. They'd be releasing him any minute now. He was fast becoming a better lawbreaker than me.

In the meantime, I was seriously in danger of having to pay for an additional night, as the desk clerk was beginning to look impatient at my unwillingness to leave. We still hadn't vacated the room. I realized I might have to pack Bateman's boxer shorts myself, but I wasn't too concerned; I knew most of them had never been worn.

Minutes later an old and battered town car pulled up outside the motel with Bateman in the passenger seat, a woman in the driver's seat, and a small dog perched in the back. The fact that the car had no siren or lights told me that he had not spent the night in jail and that his night's sleep had in fact been somewhere much more comfortable than a cell.

"Where the hell have you been?" I asked quite loudly. "Checkout time was over an hour ago."

Bateman's eyes were glazed over and his hair was scruffy, but nonetheless he managed to produce a sound explanation of the events that had unfolded.

"After the club, I got into some car and went to a party. There was this house with a big, angry dog tied up and it had plenty of beer, so I was happy. Then we all got kicked out and some guy told me a story about a shooting. Then I went back to the old bird's house. Her name was Crystal. Never did stop taking the piss out of that name."

"Right. Anyway, we're ready to go."

Fontanelle was now well within our sights, and as we turned off the interstate, we made our way south onto Nebraska Route 72, which we hoped would carry us the twenty or so miles to the town. After no further than a mile on the small, straight single-lane road with endless fields on either side, we felt as if interstate travel was a million miles away and we were as good as nowhere. Every intersecting road we came to was as straight and true as our own, and the grid-pattern-style designs that feature in most of America's cities was being replicated on a grander and more rural scale. As our road first descended into the rolling green pastures and then rose to reveal much more of the same, a sign for Fontanelle was visible, and we took the required right onto a road that fluctuated over the fields and plains but remained firmly and eternally at 90 degrees to the road we had just left and exactly parallel to the roads that sprouted from other junctions. I looked at the map and discovered that most roads in America's Midwest are laid out this way. With flat, open land on which to build roads, builders had no obstacles to avoid and so simply made them direct, leaving the map looking more like the layout of a circuit board or the pipeline screensaver I once had on my computer.

I'm sure the 675 people who inhabit Fontanelle love living there, but from my first impressions of the town I can't think why. It's a town in the middle of a collection of huge fields in the middle of a state in the middle of the country. In whatever direction you choose to leave, you're presented with the same thing—nothing. It may not have been an Arizona desert town, miles from civilisation and yards from cacti, but to me, Fontanelle, a speck amongst meadows and endless flat greenery, seemed just as isolated. I parked the car and entered a local shop located on Main Street—a totally undeserved and unjustified title that made a mockery of other Main Streets around the world. Taking four quarters out of my wallet, I walked over to the pay phone and rang Lee.

"Hello?" shouted Lee over the noise of car engines.

"Where are you to?" I asked, adding the completely un-necessary but Cornish *to* to the end of the question.

"At the racetrack. Where are you?" he replied without the *to*. This new American accent of his must have removed all the Cornishisms in him.

"In Fontanelle. You should see this place. My God. Can we get this thing over and done with, please? Where's Jen?"

"She's at home. Ring me back in about forty-five minutes and she'll sort it out for you."

"Right. I'll try to amuse myself until then," I replied. "I'll check out the sights."

Forty-five minutes was going to be hard to pass in a town of this size, but as I returned to the car and placed the key in the ignition, I was sure that a slow and detailed look around the town would do the trick. Jen had told me that the shop was the hub of the town, and going by the three people in the vicinity of the shop at that time, she was correct. We pulled out slowly onto Main Street and instantly passed an old, shabby hut on our right that turned out to be the Fontanelle town hall. A quick right revealed the town's water tower, and the house immediately after landmark number two was the highlight of our self-guided tour—a man had converted his garage into a bar, and his only customer appeared to be himself. He seemed to be enjoying every moment of his lonesome debauchery. Another corner and we were back on Main Street and again in the parking space we had vacated four minutes earlier.

Thirty long minutes later, my impatience sent me back into the shop to phone Lee again.

"Hi, Lee. Any luck with Jen and her mates?" I asked.

"Not really, mate. She's tried a few but they all say no."

"I don't blame them. They must have seen a picture of me somehow."

"Just go out on the street and find one," Lee suggested.

"Lee, have you actually been to Fontanelle? There is nothing and no one here. It's awful. How could Jen have lived here?" I replied.

"Right, I'm handing you over to Jen."

"I've tried a few numbers, but no one seems to be up for it. Loads of them are pregnant, remember?" said Jen when she took the phone.

"OK, but the only reason I'm here is because of you," I replied, deliberately putting pressure on her.

Suddenly the phone went dead. I held the phone close to my ear but could hear nothing. I was about to hang up, but then heard a ringing noise.

"You still there?" asked Jen.

"Yeah—what are we doing? How can the phone be ringing? Is this like a three-way call or something?" I asked frantically as the phone was answered and ringing ceased.

"Yes. Now shush and let me talk."

I held the phone close to my ear and listened in absolute silence as Jen spoke to the mother of one of her old friends. I heard the mother say she didn't know her daughter's new number and so the conversation ended.

"You still there, Rich?" Jen asked.

"Yep. What are we gonna do?"

"Don't worry. It's easy. Just go over to my other friend's house. She'll do it."

"Is she pregnant?" I enquired.

"Um . . . yes, I think so. OK, I'll give you the address. Then all you have to do is speak to her mother."

This really wasn't going to work. "Her mother? What am I going to say to her? 'Hiya, you don't know me but can I kiss your daughter for more than five minutes because it's illegal to in Iowa?' No way. That would be the action of a madman," I snapped. "Don't you know anyone else?"

"Nope, sorry. Everyone's changed their number or doesn't really want to do it."

"OK, then. Thanks anyway," I replied.

Another failure. But the first time I didn't feel any remorse or disappointment. Failure here meant I was free to leave Fontanelle, which was definitely not a negative. I felt as liberated as Patrick McGoohan after escaping Portmeirion on the final episode of *The Prisoner*, or as Tim Robbins' character as he stood in the rain outside the perimeter of Shawshank Penitentiary.

Back on I-80, Bateman had spotted a dead deer on the side of the road, meaning I definitely needed to spot a dinosaur in order to win the game. Eventually we pulled over at a bar for an evening meal.

The Sportts Bar (yes, two *t*'s) was as typical of an American restaurant as it gets. Tables situated by the windows seemed attached to the walls. Seating consisted of tough, plastic curves, which meant a shuffle down to the end of the bench was required. I was intrigued by the two-pound Sumo Burger Challenge. If you finished it, you won a T-shirt. It was mighty tempting to try and seemed a more alluring prospect than the rather cheap "Cup-a-Soup of the day." Behind us sat seven men, all dressed in regulation baseball caps, jeans, and checked shirts, looking like extras from *The Dukes of Hazzard*. I glanced back at the menu. I realized I had missed too many Friday fish and chips days whilst over in America, and that was one law I wasn't happy to be breaking. It wasn't a Friday, but fish and chips it would have to be.

When I paid for the meal at the counter, I couldn't help asking the cashier, who had her hair in a bun with a pencil pushed through (all she needed was a jug of coffee in her hand and a cigarette hanging from her mouth), why the word *Sportts* was spelt with two *t*'s.

"Was it a typo by the sign maker and then you had to label everything with it?" I asked.

The waitress looked puzzled. "No, it's just a name that sticks in your head," she replied.

It was a typo.

I-80 carried us over the mighty Mississippi River, confirming we had entered eastern America. Chicago grew ever nearer. Gently sloped, tree-covered hills met the riverbanks, and the Mississippi radiated a powerful, all-encompassing presence. Of course, all this escaped me, as earlier I'd seen a sign that read: "Deer—Next 10 Miles." My eyes were firmly watching the road. Being so far behind in the roadkill game, it was eyes down for a full house.

9

Bateman lives four miles from my home. I live in a coastal village, and he lives in the closest town, called Redruth. For many years now, the "Welcome to Redruth" sign has included details stating that the town is twinned with a place called Mineral Point in Wisconsin. I had always promised myself that if I was ever within a hundred miles of Mineral Point—not thinking it was anything but a very remote possibility—then I would drop in to visit. To Mineral Point from Madison, where we stayed the previous night, was a distance under fifty miles, which seemed like nothing by now. We had a couple of spare days due to the cheese factory fiasco, and it seemed very unbrotherly of us to not visit our twin when we were so close.

Strangely lettered roads led the way to Mineral Point after we left the interstate, and things began to get very confusing. The junction of the K road, leading to Hollandale, was later followed by the HHH, QQ, and G. We managed to arrive in Mineral Point and parked on what appeared to be the main street. I stepped out of the car and surveyed my surroundings, looking for telltale signs of similarities between Redruth and this small town in the middle of Wisconsin. I didn't see too many. Mineral Point was deathly quiet, I couldn't see any old ladies randomly talking to each other in the road, and I couldn't see a single kebab or charity shop. The street, which we later discovered was called High Street, was at least similar in size to Redruth's Fore Street. It contained no more than fifty or so storefronts, and we slowly made our way down the sidewalk in order to find the local information centre. We passed an astronomically large number of antiques shops and galleries—many more than you'd expect to survive in a town of only 3,000 residents, and many, many times more than you'd see in Redruth, where the profanity scrawled on the side of boarded-up buildings with smashed windows is the closest thing you'd get to art. After only a minute of walking we were nearing the halfway mark of High Street. I stopped the only lady in the street and asked her for directions.

"Excuse me, we're from Redruth and—" The mere mention of the word sent the woman into a handshaking frenzy, and she gripped my hand with more strength than I had thought a person of her age and size could muster.

"Oh, really? Very pleased to meet you. Welcome to Mineral Point," she replied, still shaking my hand in what appeared to be an attempt to break it off to keep as a souvenir.

"Thanks. I was wondering if you knew where the local information centre was in Mineral Point," I asked, hoping her shaking hand was also her pointing one too.

"The Chamber of Commerce, right there," she replied, pointing to a building only thirty yards from us and finally releasing my right hand from its vigorous roller-coaster ride of a handshake. "Yeah, Joy'll help you out with all you need to know."

We thanked the lady and made our way across the road to the Mineral Point Chamber of Commerce. Joy Gieseke, as her card explained, was the executive director of the Chamber, and after we explained where we were from, she was just as pleased to meet us as the lady in the street was—minus the handshake ordeal. Courtesy of Joy and her abundant array of brochures and information booklets, I began to learn much more about Mineral Point. The Redruth connection stems from the town's mining heritage. The discovery of lead gave rise to a mineral rush. Word travelled fast, and prospectors rushed to the town, including settlers who came from as far afield as Cornwall. The town's Cornish links are still visible to this day, as typically American timber-frame houses stand alongside limestone and sandstone buildings constructed by the early immigrants. Most of Joy's brochures seemed to feature Pendarvis Mine as Mineral Point's main attraction. Pendarvis was also the name of a tin mine just miles from my home, and Joy, noticing my interest in the site tour, handed me a piece of pink paper.

"That's a free ticket for the tour. Sorry, I only have one," she said, turning to Bateman. "So what's Redruth like?"

Bateman and I stared at each other, both wondering what the most polite and euphemistic way of saying "shithole" was. Bateman's brain clicked into gear.

"Well, it's better than Camborne. That's just full of teenage pregnancies."

"And thugs," I added. We hoped that painting a crude picture of Camborne might make it seem like Redruth was the nicer place to live. I didn't want Joy thinking badly of her twin town.

"Well, we've had some of the high school kids over here. The two schools do an exchange every few years or so. They seem to enjoy it," remarked Joy, who seemed to be playing it safe as well.

"Talking of Camborne, does Mineral Point have any local rivals, like Redruth and Camborne?" Bateman asked.

"Well, there's always been a rivalry with Dodgeville, just down the road."

"As Cornishmen, we shall take them as our common enemy too then," I said.

We sat down at a handsome oak tree table that was situated in the centre of the room, and Joy produced a map of the town to show us more of Mineral Point and where we would have to go for the Pendarvis tour. I was fascinated by the layout of the town.

"It's not a grid pattern," I said with maybe too much excitement in my voice. Most maps of towns in this country resemble potato waffles.

"Yeah, we're very proud of that here," Joy replied.

"It's a wonderful random mess of roads. It's great. No roundabouts, though." Maybe I needed to get over the roundabout thing.

"I love roundabouts," Joy replied with a smile on her face. "There's one in Dodgeville, I believe."

"Is there?" I replied in surprise, instantly ruing the pact I had made to hate Dodgeville just seconds before.

We remained in the Chamber for quite some time and learned some bizarre facts about our twin town. Wisconsin's state nickname, the Badger State, was first conceived in this area, named after the early settlers' crude shelters, which were known as "badger holes"; the town had nearly become the state capital but had lost to Madison by a single vote; and more than fifty artists, artisans, authors, musicians, and performing artists reside in Mineral Point. Bateman and I, however, were interested in more important matters.

"Is there anywhere we can get a pasty?" I asked.

"Well, the Red Rooster is only just down the road. I've heard they make very nice pasties."

Bateman and I scoffed at her suggestion. "We'll be the judges of that," we said in almost perfect unison.

"As much as I like you, Joy, I can't take an American's advice on what a good pasty is," I said jokingly.

"After you've been there, come back here and I'll introduce you to Carole Rule and her husband. Norman is probably one of the most Cornish people in Mineral Point, I would imagine."

I wondered what she meant by that.

At Joy's suggestion, Bateman and I took another walk down the empty main street of the town, arriving at the door of the Red Rooster. The quiet, vacant feel of the town was less present here, due to renovation work currently in progress. Scaffolding and ladders lay propped up against the wall, and the entire town's population seemed to be enjoying a meal inside.

Petrol, fast food, and nearly everything else may be cheaper in America, but as I studied the restaurant's menu, I discovered that pasties certainly weren't, and begrudgingly searched for $5 in my wallet. A pasty, which basically is meat and vegetables wrapped up in a crimped piece of pastry, is as quintessentially Cornish as mining and fishing. But there was certainly no coast in which to catch a couple of mackerel anywhere near Mineral Point, so I was very curious to see how the fare in town compared to that of its Cornish cousin. After ordering my food, I waited with bated breath. When the pasty finally arrived, I made some rather disturbing discoveries. Firstly, the pasty had arrived in a polystyrene box, not a bag, to which I was accustomed. Secondly, I had been presented with a fork with which to eat it. Furthermore, after lifting the lid to judge the pasty on its presentation, I discovered it had no crimp and resembled a deflated scone. Lastly, and most alarmingly, the waitress handed me a polystyrene condiment container.

"And here's your chilli sauce, sir," she said quite cheerfully.

"My what? Did you say chilli sauce? What do I want that for?" I replied disapprovingly, pushing the container back along the counter in her direction. "How dare you," I added in jest.

But the proof of the pasty is, of course, in the eating. I picked the pasty up from out of its box and took a bite.

Bateman looked on expectantly. "What's it like?"

"Um . . . different," I replied. It wasn't so much the ingredients that were wrong with the pasty; it was the texture and taste. It was dry and quite stodgy, and I almost regretted declining the chilli sauce—a difficult thing for a Cornishman to admit. Disappointed and still very hungry, we returned to the Chamber to berate Joy for ever having sent us to the Red Rooster in the first place.

"How was it?" Joy asked upon our entry.

"Don't ask," I replied without expression.

Just as she had promised, Joy led us across the road to the local estate agent's, run by Carole and Norman Rule. With Rule being a very Cornish name, I had very high expectations as we entered the office. Norman Rule was an elderly gentleman with a tartan-style shirt and glasses. As I shook his hand, I was about to tell him about the woman with the vigorous handshake I'd met before. Then I saw his wife. Carole Rule was charming, incredibly affable, very welcoming, and the woman I had met in the street earlier.

"Ah, I believe we've met before," I said, keeping my hands where she couldn't get to them. (I'd learnt my lesson.)

The office was small and clean, leading me to deduce that real estate wasn't a hasty, relentless business in Mineral Point. Many maps and pictures of Cornwall covered the walls and may have even outnumbered the house advertisements in the front window. I quickly pointed out on the map where Bateman and I hailed from. I then began to question Norman on his Cornishness. Norman's ancestors, he explained, were originally from Camborne and Redruth and had come to Mineral Point as some of the first prospectors during the "mineral rush" of which I had learnt earlier. He explained the whole story whilst standing in front of a beautifully drawn painting of the 1497 Cornish Rebellion that hung on the wall beside his desk.

Joy, who had obviously forgotten about her responsibilities in the Chamber of Commerce, remained with us and after about fifteen minutes decided we should have a picture taken of us all. As we made our way out of the estate agency with our growing entourage, we sat in front of one of the numerous antiques shops while Carole captured the moment with Joy's camera.

In America, almost half the homes you see have the Stars and Stripes adorning their front porch or on a flagpole, and their cars are donned similarly. In the UK, you'd be hard pushed to see the Union Jack appearing on one in a thousand homes unless the national football team was taking part in a tournament. Our car's parcel shelf was featureless, and it needed a bit of Cornish restoration.

Returning with Joy to the Chamber of Commerce, we asked where we could buy a Cornish flag for our car. If we were ever going to find a Cornish flag in America, this would be the place.

"I'll ring Catherine for you, but I'm not sure if she's open," she replied.

"But it's one o'clock on a Tuesday afternoon," I replied incredulously. The telephone rang and rang, but no one answered. We learnt that the only shop in which a Cornish flag could be purchased opened every day of the week except Tuesdays.

"You could always try the tour shop. They might have some," Joy suggested.

Using the map Joy had given us, we made our way to the

Pendarvis tour shop. Amidst the copious amount of Cornish paraphernalia, from pencils to mugs, we found a small Cornish flag and a Union Jack. We attached both to the car's aerial. We returned to the centre of town along Shake Rag Street, a street where traditional Cornish cottages stood at the foot of hills that had once been dotted by lead mines. The road was tiny and placid, and if it hadn't been for the torturous heat, it would have definitely reminded me of home. We left the car by the side of the road for a quick photo and noticed a huge Cornish flag hanging from the entrance to the Mineral Point Living Arts Center.

"Ask if we can buy theirs off them," shouted Bateman. Thinking it was a great idea, I entered the building and walked straight into a meeting.

"Sorry to interrupt you, but I was wondering if your Cornish flag was for sale and if I could buy it off you. The shop that sells them is shut." Pleasant folks they were—they weren't the least bit annoyed that I had interrupted a meeting, and they were keen to learn about my trip around the States.

"I'll ring Catherine," said one of the ladies as she rose from her chair and made her way into the office where I was standing.

"I think you'll find she's not in," I said rather smugly, remembering the earlier phone call Joy had made. I turned my attention back to the other ladies around the table, getting ready to make an offer on their flag. Surely $30 would seal the deal.

When she returned, the woman said, "She's gonna be there in ten minutes and open the shop especially for you."

"Oh . . . thanks."

Catherine Whitford owns just a corner of a shop known as the Mineral Point Collection, and, selling all things Cornish, she unashamedly named her business the Cornish Corner.

As she approached from out of the shop's dark interior to unlock the door, I apologised profusely for interrupting her day off and thanked her for opening just for me and on such short notice.

"Oh, that doesn't matter. Tekter and I only live in the house out the back. It's not far to walk."

Trehawke's Prince Tekter (to give him his full name) is Catherine's six-year-old shih tzu, who quickly appeared, scuttled around, and smelled my legs before being swept into the arms of Catherine, who proceeded to show me around the store. Cornish plates, tin products imported from St. Just, and a fine selection of pewter, tin, and sterling silver jewellery featured in a consummate collection of everything Cornish. Catherine's family name, Trehawke, she explained, dates back to Cornwall as far back as the reign of William the Conqueror and features within the pages of the Domesday Book (the original English population census, completed by William the Conqueror in 1086). All of this was explained to me as I slowly made my way towards the shelf where the Cornish flags were found.

"So how much is that massive flag there?" I asked.

Catherine looked at me dolefully. "Well, they're quite expensive. I have to import them in from overseas. That big one is fifty-five dollars."

"Right. I'll take the medium-sized one."

The medium-sized flag was still overpriced at $35. As Catherine and I walked towards the counter to complete the transaction, I noticed that the flag in my hand had been imported from Par, near St. Austell. To put this in context, I was paying about £20 for a piece of cloth I could have bought for £10 just down the road from my home. As I handed over the cash, Bateman entered the shop and joined us.

"Oh, and is this your friend?" asked Catherine.

"Yes. He's the reason I'm buying it, really," I replied.

"Take a few postcards if you want," she added, pointing at a revolving rack on the counter. "And you must be missing tea. Have these tea bags."

Catherine's generosity was like nothing I had ever experienced before. Not only had she opened the shop especially for us on her day off, but now she was searching around her counter for extras to add to my flag purchase.

"Oh, take more postcards than that. Have three or four," she demanded, thrusting extra cards into a brown paper bag she had produced to place the goodies in. "Oh, how rude of me. Have these Jaffa Cakes too."

Bateman and I had only planned on a quick browse around Mineral Point, but the warm greeting we received, plus the generous and friendly people we had met, minus the pasty we had eaten, added up to a feeling of belonging even though we were thousands of miles from home. Here I experienced an affectionate sense of family and kinship. It was now getting on for four o'clock, and we decided it was too late to make our way to Chicago, so we used the free tour ticket I had received earlier in the day and drove to Pendarvis for the final tour of the day.

Bateman and I, along with eight other people, waited patiently for the tour to begin. Maps of Cornwall, pictures of the county, and a portrait of Robert Neal adorned the room in which we were asked to wait. Neal was the man who had preserved the Pendarvis cottage at a time when miners were tearing down stone dwellings for their materials in the 1930s. Without Neal, the tour of the cottage would not have been possible. As people checked their watches with increasing anxiety for the tour to begin, I hadn't ruled out the fact that one of the waiting group members could in fact be our guide. I studied the leading candidates. An elderly couple sat in the corner. They hadn't spoken since we walked in, not even to each other; maybe they were saving their breath to conduct a tour. In front of them stood a small man with glasses, who appeared to be unaccompanied; perhaps *he* was getting ready to round up his respective clients. Outside stood a woman in an early 1900s nightgown and bonnet. She wouldn't have looked out of place sitting in a rocking chair on the front of her porch, defending her ranch with a shotgun. Out of the three candidates, I decided she had to be the favourite.

The tour turned out to be of the preserved cottages and their surroundings rather than the mine itself, and there was a lot of talk about the lives of the miners. As we were led through the small granite homes and talked through the settlers' lives, our bonneted guide insisted on clarifying every fact with me, as if my Cornish upbringing had put me in a position to serve as some kind of supervisor. I, of course, was no wiser than the rest of the group.

"The Cornish first made pies with fish in them, didn't they?"

"I don't know. I had a pasty today, though, and it wasn't great. Does that help?"

The tour continued. Entering one of the granite homes gave us our only chance to hide from the sun. Because of the relentless heat, when the tour finally ended as all tours do— in the gift shop—all of the members felt a huge sense of relief, none more so than me. I had to get back to the car; I'd left the Jaffa Cakes in there.

We returned to the Chamber one final time and bid farewell to Joy, thanking her for her help and generosity. As a parting gift, Joy presented us each with a Mineral Point T-shirt and wished us luck for the remainder of our trip.

We were due to finally arrive in Chicago the following day, and although we were now more than halfway through the trip distance-wise, the spree was far from over. Mineral Point had been a welcome break, but we had to get back to the criminal business at hand. America's West had not re-sulted in a great deal of lawbreaking success for me, but I felt confident about the remainder of the trip. The East con-tained more people, more towns, and, more importantly, more bizarre laws. I left Mineral Point in an upbeat mood, having made an essential purchase: a pair of pyjamas. I would need them for the strangest of all laws awaiting me in the Windy City.

10

Chicago, America's third largest city, was certainly a wake-up call. We hadn't stayed in a big metropolitan area since Salt Lake City and had certainly not experienced a city on quite the same scale since leaving Los Angeles. On the day of our arrival, the Windy City was very much overcast. Visibility was only a couple of miles or so, and the haze had descended onto the downtown area, smothering the skyscrapers and softening the otherwise dominating presence of the Sears Tower.

Any normal tourist heading toward the centre of the city might have wanted to visit Chicago's Chinatown district, tour the John Hancock Center, or take a tour on Lake Michigan to study the city's stupendous architecture. Under normal circumstances, I would have joined them, but I had a completely different sort of itinerary planned. We headed north of the city towards Montrose Harbour, a destination that probably doesn't appear on a great many tourists' to-do lists.

It is illegal in Chicago to fish in one's pyjamas. Apparently it's also illegal to catch a fish sitting on a giraffe's neck (the angler, not the fish). With pyjamas much more readily available than giraffes in department stores nowadays, I opted for the easier of the two.

The drive to the harbour turned out to be a very cultural experience. As we approached Chicago, the suburbs of leafy neighbourhood streets and shopping precincts suddenly yielded to miles of industry. Where we'd once seen houses, gardens, and the occasional park, we now encountered an ugly spectacle of cargo containers, railway lines, and dilapidated factory buildings. The smog didn't make it any prettier. Closer to the downtown area, we crossed the Chicago River, passing the city's amphitheatric Soldier Field, a stadium of almost 70,000 capacity and home to the Chicago Bears football team.

Entering Chicago's downtown area was a strangely humbling experience. To our right lay hundreds of stationary yachts bobbing docilely on the unruffled waters of Lake Michigan. To our left stood the intimidating view of corporate America—hundreds of concrete structures that had sprouted from the financially fertile land of the shore. As we drove, I looked over at the lake again to see that its complexion had changed once more. The endless harbours and rows of yachts and other sailing vessels had suddenly parted, replaced by Navy Pier, which projected deep into Lake Michigan. It featured a Ferris wheel, restaurants, and bars in an evocative reminder of the British seaside. Finally, to my surprise, a beach appeared.

Even though I was raised near the coast, the presence of a beach seemed completely surreal. Never in my life have I been so close to both people lazing on the white sands of the shore and the hustle and hurried commotion of a busy metropolis. My home is just as picturesque as the beaches on Chicago's coastline, but the nearest road with more than four lanes of traffic is over ninety miles away. In Chicago, the two are separated by just six lanes of gridlocked traffic.

My first impressions of Montrose Harbour were curious, to say the least. After parking the car and taking a look around, I noticed there were no boats, no yachts, and, rather crucially, no water. I referred to the map to see if we had arrived in the right place and discovered the harbour was situated at the end of Lincoln Park. Judging by the dozens of soccer pitches I could see over the flapping pages of the map, we must have been in Lincoln Park, just at the wrong end.

Once we had found it, we discovered that Montrose Harbour had numerous amenities, including beaches, piers, and hundreds of boats. The Windy City's law would be a breeze. Fishing opportunities abounded around the harbour's rounded shape. All I needed to do was find a quayside business that hired out rods. I could see only one. On the other side of the harbour and a good walk back in the direction of the car, another beach lay in hiding behind a concrete structure that acted as changing rooms for the beach patrons and provided an impressive archway leading to the beautiful shoreline. We stepped through the arch and onto the beach's modest promenade, which was lightly covered in sand. I looked around for the door to the hire centre. To my left stood half a dozen children, each clutching an ice cream or soft drink. To my right was exactly what I was looking for. Phew. The rental sign informed me that from this hole in the wall I could hire anything nautical, from a Jet Ski to a banana boat. On closer inspection my relief was short-lived. Sure, I could hire a Jet Ski, a kayak, a surfboard, a wet suit, and maybe a rod—if the business had not been boarded up and closed down indefinitely.

Making our way back to the harbour, and contemplating a drive into town to buy our props, I suddenly had an idea.

"I don't have to hire a rod or even buy one," I said to Bateman, who seemed to be growing ever more impatient. It was probably already beer o'clock for him. "I'll just borrow one. All I have to do is find someone who'll let me."

The harbourside was enormous, and as we walked around the perimeter we felt sure we would find a fisherman who would only be too pleased to assist us. Fifteen minutes later we had passed dozens of Americans who seemed kind and pleasant enough to fit the bill. Trouble was, they weren't fishing. The only man who was sat cross-legged staring into the water, dropping and lifting a piece of string into the sea like a yo-yo. Bateman slyly pointed to him and suggested I ask him if I could hold his string after putting on my pyjamas.

"Um, he's my number one reserve if I can't find anyone else, mate."

We had almost reached the end of the harbour, passing yachts named *Cat's Meow* and *No Inheritance,* when I discovered a bank leading to what must have been the open expanse of the lake and away from the harbour. It was there, standing at the top of the incline, that I discovered where all the fishermen had been hiding from me. From the top, several concrete steps led to a flat 20-foot breakwater before dropping into the lake. Numerous fishermen sat quayside waiting patiently with rod and cool box by their side. I noticed a man and his son were fishing just at the foot of the steps. They seemed the perfect targets, partly due to their friendly faces but mostly because they were closest and my feet were sore. We sat on the bottom step and studied our targets, wondering how best to ask. Stuff it, there wasn't an easy way, was there? Leaving my pyjamas in my rucksack, I made my way over to the father, thinking of Arden, the Native American Snap master, and applying a similar style of approach.

"Excuse me." Good start. "I have a rather bizarre request to ask of you. I'm going around America breaking strange laws, and it's illegal in Chicago to fish in your pyjamas. Now, I have some pyjamas in my bag, and all I'm really asking you is if I can hold your rod. I don't need to catch anything, just be seen to be fishing. Is that all right?" I asked, almost gasping for air.

The man laughed and scratched his head. "Well, you're right about the bizarre request. But sure." His son, who had obviously heard the entire thing, looked on with a horrified expression, as if wondering why his dad had agreed to the madman's request.

"All right, mate?" I asked the boy, to try to calm his nerves.

"Fine, thanks," he replied, turning his attention back to the water.

I walked back to my rucksack and began to change into my nightwear. "Wait until you see my pyjamas. These are great."

The pyjamas, which were a few sizes too big for me, were the traditional collared, button-up kind, grey with hundreds of navy blue motifs similar to badly drawn snowflakes. My new friends, Bill Stover and his ten-year-old son, David, looked a little more concerned now that they had actually seen I wasn't winding them up. So did the other fishermen.

"Right, I'm ready."

Bill had reeled in his line. He must have wanted me to do this properly.

"You know how to cast off, don't you?" he asked whilst pointing at the reel.

"I think so. I hold on to the line and flick this thing-amajig," I replied, showing off my knowledge of fishing terminology.

"That's right."

After a simple but effective cast, the law had been broken. I didn't have to catch anything; I simply had to fish. David, who by now was standing a good distance away from me, gazed out to sea, taking no notice of what I was doing. Maybe this sort of thing had happened to him before. I reeled the line back in, having caught nothing, and handed the rod back to his dad.

"Thanks, Bill. You've been a great help."

"Where are you off to next on this adventure?" he asked.

"Well, we're here for a couple more days, and then we're travelling south to Indianapolis."

"You do this by public transport?"

"No, hire car. It would be very difficult in this country to travel by public trans . . ." I looked down at what I was wearing.

"Hey, Bill, maybe I should get changed before I begin a discussion about the inadequacy of America's public transportation. You mind?"

I returned to my bag, changed, and shook Bill's hand for a second time. He made a wonderful attempt of relating to my adventure.

"Hey. I'm not sure if it's illegal, but I once cross-country skied across the Buckingham Fountain when I was younger," he said.

"Really? We passed that. It's quite impressive. I'm pretty sure it would be illegal."

As I thanked Bill and David, shaking their hands and promising I would leave them alone, I noticed David was wearing a Chicago Cubs T-shirt.

"You a Cubs fan, then?" I asked him, in a last ditch attempt to prove I wasn't a simple-minded idiot.

"Yeah."

"We might go and see them in the next couple of days."

"You can't. They're playing in Seattle."

"Oh, right." As if the boy needed more proof of my idiocy.

So the Cubs weren't playing at home in the next few days.

We had to see a game while we were in town—baseball is America's national sport! Luckily I knew that Chicago had two baseball teams. The Chicago White Sox were definitely in town and playing that afternoon. Thanking Bill and David one final time, we headed to the White Sox's stadium. We had a lovely afternoon of no lawbreaking and family-friendly entertainment planned. What harm could possibly come to us?

U.S. Cellular Field, located a few miles south of the downtown area, is the home of the Chicago White Sox. The excitement of fishing had tired me out, and I simply wanted to sit down amongst thousands of fans, watch a game, and try to learn the rules of baseball. I figured the game's nine innings of play would give me plenty of time to get my head round the sport.

Two-thirty on a Thursday afternoon seemed a rather strange time to me to stage a baseball game, but by the looks of the full-to-capacity parking lots and queues of people in White Sox shirts lining up behind the many ticket windows, it seemed only the fans of the Chicago Cubs were at work today. It's probably due to the length of the games that not one of the hundreds of fans who found themselves still outside seemed at all concerned that the game against the Toronto Blue Jays had begun thirty minutes before they arrived. We joined the back of the shortest line and waited to reserve a seat in the crowd for the following day's evening game. The ubiquitous ticket scalpers surrounded the windows, offering their tickets to passersby and anyone who was waiting patiently in line. Their sales skills proved useless against my stone-wall-like defence.

"I've got two tickets for upper reserved or bleachers. You want?"

"No thanks, mate. I don't have a clue what you're talking about."

When we finally reached the front of the queue and asked for the price of a ticket to the evening game the following day, we were informed that the only seats they had left to sell were upper-tier seats with obscured view—affectionately referred to by all American sports fans as the nosebleed seats. Ultimately, the humidity and temperature put Bateman and me off watching the afternoon game, for which tickets were still available, and we settled for returning to the car, deciding to watch a game in New York or Boston later in our trip.

Leaving the ballpark and travelling east back to our motel on city streets, we seemed to have entered one of the roughest parts of the city. Litter covered the sidewalks, and every convenience store used iron bars to protect their windows and business. As I drove through the streets, trying not to make eye contact with anyone for fear of a gangland attack, a car coming from the opposite direction attempted to turn left across my path as I approached.

"What was he doing?" shouted Bateman. "It was our right of way."

It wasn't long until we heard a police siren loud and clear—or deafening and irritating, you could also say. I was waiting at a junction at the time and looked left and right in order to allow the police, wherever they were, to continue in their pursuit quickly and efficiently.

"Where's that coming from?" I asked Bateman. "It's not anywhere down there."

"It's not behind us—there's just a normal car there," he replied.

We continued for a couple more blocks and heard the siren for a second time. Once again, the cops were nowhere to be seen; we assumed they had turned off towards the scene of the crime, and we continued. By now, we must have driven half a mile or so after hearing the siren for the first time, and we grew concerned when the same noise was heard for a third time. This time, however, it was much more intense and sounded closer. Looking to my left, I noticed that the blue car that had been behind us had accelerated and was now positioned alongside. There were three men in it. The man travelling in the front passenger seat demanded I pull over, and without thinking I stopped the car and turned the engine off. The only thing going through my mind was that it was a gang member's car. Perhaps they used the siren to pose as undercover policemen before they robbed you and took your vehicle. I was prepared to quickly drive away again, but the seconds I had wasted while thinking of this worst possible outcome had given the three men enough time to quickly jump out of their car and surround both the front doors of our vehicle. The fact they were wearing bulletproof vests made me fearful enough, but I hadn't decided if the fact that they had them on was a good thing or a bad thing. Bateman suddenly opened his door to see what the problem was. This was a big mistake.

"Show me your hands! Show me your hands!" demanded one of the men, who by now had one hand straight in front of him and the other resting on the gun in his holster. Bateman had no choice but to agree. He showed his right hand to be empty and his left hand to hold a Chicago sightseeing guide. Meanwhile, I was having my own problems—I had two guys on my side.

"Open your window! Open your window!"

With utter confusion running through my head coupled with the fact that I had nearly soiled myself in the buildup to the ordeal, I lost all knowledge of how to operate a car window.

"Do it now!" screamed the cop.

I quickly remembered the windows were electric and after

turning the key to allow power to the car—simultaneously miming that I wasn't going to drive away—managed successfully to comply with the demand. I made sure to remain in my seat and make no sudden movements, especially not to open my door. That had worked out very poorly for Bateman. The cop stood sternly.

"Were you ever planning on stopping at those stop signs?"

Time to play ignorant. "Stop signs, Officer? I didn't see any. Did you, Bateman?" Bateman shook his head.

"Well, you run two of them back there. Almost causing an accident at the first." I didn't want to point out that *run* was grammatically incorrect.

"Did I? Well, I'm terribly sorry. I'm from England and still getting used to the roads here."

The mention of England seemed to relax the cop. His whole posture and pattern of speech loosened. He turned to his colleague behind him, smiled, and gestured towards us. "They're from England."

Cop number three, who hadn't spoken a word up to this point and who was bizarrely sporting a marijuana medallion, leant in front of his partner and up to my window. "G'day!"

Maybe he should stick to being the quiet, daunting type.

My ignorance and nationality apparently proved my innocence, but the cops, now much more relaxed, looked in through my windows to where the pyjamas rested on the backseat.

"What's that flag in the back?" one asked.

"It's a Cornish flag."

"Cornish? What's that?"

"We're from a part of England called Cornwall, and that's its flag."

"Cornwall?"

I decided not to lecture the man with the gun.

"It's an English flag, OK?"

"Oh, an English flag. I get ya. 'Cause you're from England, right? Anyway, where you headed?"

"Trying to get back to the interstate."

"It's straight up and then make a left."

With that taken care of, the three men who held us at gunpoint joyfully helped us back to the freeway and didn't even ask about the pajamas. Obviously, driving through a few stop signs was a far more serious crime than fishing in your PJs.

That evening in the Kerry Piper Irish Bar, just yards from our motel, quiz night was well under way when Bateman and I sat down in the only two empty chairs we could find. A throng of people awaited each question, which the quizmaster yelled from just behind where we were sitting.

Across from us was a team with only two members, and they didn't appear to be doing too well. Joey and his partner, Jackie, were both music teachers and worked at a middle school south of Chicago, as we found out while chatting during the break. When the second half of the quiz commenced, I gave them a bit of a hand if I had an inkling of the answer, shaking my head and shrugging at any question involving an American sport. Given how confident the other teams seemed, and that our combined specialisation in music and bizarre American laws was probably not a formula for victory, it was clear we were a team destined for failure.

"How was Edward Teach better known?" That question seemed to quieten the crowd.

"I reckon it's Blackbeard the pirate. I think I've heard it somewhere. What have you put down?" I asked Joey encouragingly.

"Edward Scissorhands," Jackie replied. Yep, I was right about our chances.

The best I could muster for the remainder of the quiz were

stupid answers and educated guesses. When the results of the quiz were revealed, it was clear that, other than the Edward Teach question, the only thing I had gotten completely and categorically correct was that we were always destined for defeat.

It was nearing closing time, and as Bateman joined Joey and Jackie at the piano onstage, I got to chatting with the quizmaster and the members of the team who'd sat behind us (and who'd beaten us quite convincingly). When I revealed the nature of my trip, Ann Traczek and the other members of her team seemed overjoyed with the whole idea.

"Well, there're plenty of them," she remarked. "It sounds like fun. Where are you going next?"

I realised Ann was a remarkably intelligent woman when she revealed her love for English soccer and Manchester United. Her husband supported Arsenal, while the rest of her team were Liverpool fans. I liked her instantly when she immediately corrected herself: "Sorry, around you I should say football."

We talked until we were asked to leave, and before we parted company, I informed Ann of our adventures that afternoon and told her I couldn't get my head around how dramatically the mood of the encounter had changed as soon as we revealed our Englishness. It had begun at gunpoint and ended just minutes later with a pleasant discussion about flags and very helpful directions leading us back to our motel. Ann nodded, not at all surprised at what had happened. Our Cornish flag, a white cross on a black background, was similar to the emblem of the Black Gangster Disciples, one of the biggest and most violent gangs in Chicago.

11

Although it wasn't an absolute necessity to wake up so stupidly early in the morning on the day when we were going to change our car and drive to Indianapolis, BBC Radio Cornwall provided my wake-up call.

I had originally promised to keep in touch with many of the local and national radio stations regarding my progress in America, but with the time difference making early-morning interviews a menace, I decided to stay loyal to my local BBC radio station and agreed to do one interview with David White of Radio Cornwall. Shortly before six in the morning, my hotel phone began to ring, and before I even realised what country I was in, the receiver was next to my ear and I was talking live to David and his discerning listeners.

"Hi, Rich. How're things going? How many laws are you up to?" he asked ebulliently.

"Well, it's not even six o'clock here, Dave, so you must bear with me."

After telling about the laws in Globe and Salt Lake City, and the pyjamas the previous day, I began to explain so poorly about the spot of bother that running a stop sign had dropped us into that soon even I didn't know what I was talking about.

"Well, you seem to be having fun. How's your friend?" he asked, saving me the embarrassment of digging myself into a deeper hole.

"Funny you should ask, actually. His name is Luke Bateman, and apparently your parents used to babysit him. Are your parents called Anne and Alex?"

"Oh, yeah, I know him."

A couple of amusing anecdotes later, Cornwall needed to hear the region's news, and I could pull the sheet back over my head and return to my slumber.

Leaving Chicago wasn't as straightforward as normal. Usually, we would consult the map and make our way in whatever direction the next law took us, but before we left the Windy City, we had to figure out how to change our hire car, as the three-week lease had expired. The car company would not allow us to take the same car for such a long time and to a destination as far as New York, and so we had to change over in Chicago if we wanted to continue driving to the Big Apple.

Luckily, the rental company's base in Chicago was at Midway International Airport, not the city's monolithic O'Hare International, which is Chicago's, America's, and the world's busiest airport. No party or celebration greeted us on the completion of the first leg of our journey, just a simple low-key "park it there" as we pulled into the second floor of a multi-storey car park that acted as the pickup and drop-off point for four rental companies. As Bateman enquired as to where we would have to go to sign the paperwork and pay for our next car, I took a look around the vehicles available for hire and, remembering the words of Brenda the psychic, hoped for a small number of red ones.

Bateman returned and must have noticed my peculiar behaviour of peering around concrete pillars in order to get a better view, because he enquired as to what I was doing.

"Nothing much. Just looking at what we might get."

"You're looking for a red one, aren't you? You really believed that woman."

"No, I'm just seeing if there are any good ones. That's all."

"I've already looked. That Jeep appears to be the only red vehicle here anyway," he said, pointing at a Jeep Wrangler parked in the corner.

Phew.

After getting lost in a stairwell and finally taking the lift, we found ourselves in the baggage collection area, where the rental companies' kiosks were and where we were greeted by a delightfully pleasant young woman.

"Hi! How can I help you?"

"Good afternoon. We've just dropped off our car and we're here to pick up another. It's reserved under the name Smith."

The desk clerk looked away and glanced at her screen for a few seconds, typing occasionally.

"And you're taking the car to New York City?"

"Yes."

"And you do know there's a drop-off charge for that?"

"Yep."

She stared at the screen once again. "And your quoted price was . . ." She gasped. "Oh, that *is* expensive, isn't it?"

"Yeah, it's because we're not twenty-five." Which is true. In America you are at a serious disadvantage for not reaching that age regardless of whether you've just passed your test or not. Strange for a country that allows people behind the wheel of a car at sixteen.

"Well, I can give you a free upgrade if you want."

This was great news. The car we had reserved was the smallest kind they had, and Bateman had already threatened to refuse a car if it turned out to be similar in size to a Ford Fiesta or Mini Metro.

"I can offer you a Jeep."

Bateman smiled and leant forward. "A Jeep? It doesn't happen to be red, does it?"

The lady glanced back at her screen, pressed a few keys, and smiled. "It does, actually. How did you know that?"

"Just a hunch." Bateman turned and stared at me, leaning on the counter. "Shall we get the *red* Jeep, then?" he remarked smugly.

I guess there's nothing wrong with accepting the Jeep, I thought. It was certainly red, but how would I look if I took the words of some crackpot seriously? A Jeep isn't even a car, really.

"OK, let's take it," I said decisively.

"Although a Jeep isn't the best form of vehicle to do another five thousand miles in, is it?" Bateman mused.

"No, course not. Let's not take it."

A lucky escape. I wasn't scared; of course I wasn't. I'd been fully prepared to accept the Jeep until Bateman voiced his concern over the vehicle's comfort for such a long journey. I turned to the clerk to show my nonchalant and unruffled machismo.

"I've upgraded you to a Dodge Neon," she remarked as she tore the receipt from out of the printer.

"What colour's that?"

Our Dodge Neon, a shade of turquoise and definitely without any hint of red, had miles already on the clock and certainly didn't compare to the Sebring. Its beige interior failed to impress, and the stains on the passenger seat made us feel as if we had borrowed the car from a not particularly hygienic friend. But as we pulled away from the airport and onto the freeway, the car revealed its similarity to the Sebring: when the accelerator pedal was firmly pushed to the floor, the car would respond by making as much noise as possible without actually increasing in speed. Bateman wasn't as annoyed as I would how expected, and the reason soon became apparent: this car had a cigarette lighter.

Indianapolis is a clean, neat, and unobtrusive city. The uncluttered streets and roads that allow the city's traffic to proceed effortlessly were a refreshing change from my experience in other American cities. But then again, the city isn't even a century old.

When Indiana became the nineteenth state in 1816, its capital was a small town called Corydon. This, however, was only a temporary measure, and by 1825 the state required a permanent capital. Only four years after Indianapolis was laid out, it was selected. It was clear that the city had been planned for the specific purpose of housing government buildings. Although the city's downtown area was similar to that of any other American metropolis, with high-rise buildings towering above well-known retailers and fast-food outlets, its central business district seemed to have been scaled down. Our motel, on its own in a flat and sparse area surrounded by disused car parks, stood by a road that seemed to have penetrated the skyscrapers and forged a gateway leading to the Monument Circle roundabout in the heart of the city.

The Soldiers and Sailors Monument stands as the centrepiece of Monument Circle and, with its towering obelisk, artistic sculpture, and fountains, is as impressive a structure as any I've seen in Europe. It would also most definitely appear if a series entitled *America's Greatest Roundabouts* was ever made.

The 230-foot tower was dedicated in 1902 to all of Indiana's heroes who had died in battles prior to World War I. After circling the tower on foot once and seeing all the names, I was surprised at how often Indiana was called into action. Soldiers lost in the 1861–65 Civil War, 1846–48

Mexican-American War, the War of 1812, and even the Revolutionary War and Vincennes' capture from the British in 1779 covered all four sides of the monument. I wasn't here for a history lesson, however. I was standing in the centre of the city in order to locate the Emmis Communications Building, which stood at 40 Monument Circle. There was no law to break there. Basically, I had travelled 200 miles out of my way because I simply wanted to meet a man whose name was Wank.

When I'd first spoken to Ed Wank and his co-host, Dave O'Brien, back in February, I had promised that I would keep in touch with them concerning the progress of my trip. I'd kept my word, and though I childishly still found Wank's name very, very amusing, I was going to appear on their breakfast show the following day. Now that I knew where the building was, I didn't have to wake up so early.

Thinking Ed and Dave would probably ask what laws pertained to Indiana and, more importantly, its capital, when we returned to our room I immediately rummaged through my bag and found my book of laws, where I discovered that in South Bend it is illegal for a monkey to smoke cigarettes. Reading the history of the law in more detail, I discovered the ape in question stood trial, was found guilty, and was ordered to pay a $25 fine as well as the cost of the trial.

I also found out that pi, known throughout the world as 3.14159265358979323846264338327950288841972 (to forty decimal places), in Indiana is simply known as 4. This law makes finding the circumference and area of circles a lot easier throughout the state, but surely the best way to simplify the sum and produce still incorrect but marginally more accurate results would be to round it down to 3.

Just for the radio show the following day, I found a suitable law that was relevant to the entire state and one I could easily break that evening.

"Let's go to the cinema, Bateman."

"Why? What's on?"

"I dunno. But it's illegal to ride on a streetcar or enter a cinema or theatre within three hours of eating garlic. I'm going to break the law, seeing as we're here. Do you know where I can get some garlic? I'm gonna eat a whole head."

"You're going to eat an entire head of garlic? You'll die," Bateman warned. "Just one clove is bad enough."

"I'm not even sure if I like garlic, actually."

I picked up the phone and asked for a pizza to be delivered to our room, making sure to ask for lots of garlic bread. Bateman looked on.

"You ain't sitting anywhere near me in the cinema."

I managed to eat two rather large pieces of garlic bread along with some chicken-topped pizza before we made our way to the cinema complex, located in the mall a couple of blocks from Monument Circle. The cinema was a multiplex with an immense list of movies showing. Unfortunately, they all seemed a bit dull, and there was nothing I was particularly keen to see. In the end, Bateman and I found ourselves in a 470-seat cinema with only nine other people watching *The Dukes of Hazzard*.

I was glad when the film was over. My memories of a perfectly good 1980s TV series were now tarnished beyond repair by how poor the movie was. Not even the legs of Jessica Simpson as Daisy Duke could save a movie that stank as badly as my breath. Bateman, who had any of the other 469 seats to choose from, had placed himself in a seat just four from my own, thinking, I guess, that would be far away enough. He seemed to enjoy the movie but not the company.

"I can still bloody smell you from here!"

● ● ●

At seven o'clock the following morning, my alarm clock
woke me. Stepping into the shower, I realised seven was the
earliest I had gotten out of bed on the entire holiday. As I left
somewhat bleary-eyed for the radio station, I read on a sign
that the gravel car park opposite our motel had in fact been
the venue for Elvis Presley's last ever concert. Fascinating.

Back in February, *The Wank and O'Brien Show* had been
the breakfast show on what was then known as Real 97.1. In
the months since, the station had shifted its format dramatically from adult contemporary to country-and-western and
now was known as Hank FM. Nearly every radio and local
television station in America is represented by a not very
memorable four-letter name and the stations that emanated
from the Emmis Communication Building proved no exception. This building housed WYXB, WNOU, WIBC, and Hank
FM (officially called WLHK). The guy who'd named the stations was probably the same idiot behind the naming of the
alphabetic roads outside Mineral Point.

I entered the building and was shown to the lift by the security guard. We were greeted by Angela, who worked on
the breakfast show as an intern. She asked us to wait in the
station's lounge and listen to the show in progress. The hosts
were in the middle of an interview with a singer named Brad
Cotter. They sounded friendly and affable, rather than being
intent on taking a pop at their guest—a quality seldom heard
in radio. From what I could make out, Brad Cotter had won
the country-and-western version of *Pop Idol* (the unimagina-
tively named *Nashville Star* and not *Pop Bridle,* which I
thought was rather more fitting) and had just released his
debut single, which he hoped would help raise money for
military families who had lost loved ones in Iraq or Afghani-
stan. Ed introduced the single, "An American Dream."

Brad's voice, similar to all singers of that ilk, sounded
powerful and inspiring and definitely reinforced the senti-

ment of the song. The song was a stirring mix of patriotism and pride in national identity, with frequent mentions of stars, stripes, and other symbolic reminders of the country. The chorus, heartfelt and rousing, was aimed at evoking the raw emotions of every proud American and kindling their passion in the virtues of the flag. I'm sure people all over the Indianapolis area were pulling their cars over to the side of the road to release the tears they could no longer hold back. I knew the song was indeed in aid of a very worthy and noble cause, but it would be instantly disliked in every country of the world but one. I don't know if any country is as defensive of its patriotism and its military as the United States.

The spacious, minimalistic layout of the lounge made me feel like Bateman and I were the first guests to arrive at a rather exclusive party. But when Brad Cotter's interview had come to an end, I realised I was definitely not the guest of honour—that accolade went to Mr. Cotter, who exited with an entourage consisting of his agent, press representatives, and numerous other associates. Though, just as I imagined he would be, he was simply dressed in jeans, a buttoned shirt, and the obligatory cowboy hat, it was obvious the man in the middle of the crowd, guitar in hand, was the Nashville star himself. As he passed our seats, he even took the time to shake my hand, and Angela formally introduced us.

"Heard your song, mate. It was really good."

I returned to my seat next to Bateman after relishing the beauty of sarcasm and the Americans' general failure to ever detect a single hint of it, and watched the singer shake hands with the station's representatives before being hurried into the lift to continue with his hectic schedule. I must admit, I felt a tad jealous of the attention and all the fuss made over him, while Bateman and I were largely ignored, but I suppose it was justified. He would soon be an international recording artist—he had places to be, people to meet, and videos to shoot. I was here simply to meet a guy with a funny name, and I probably still reeked of garlic.

The *Wank and O'Brien Show* broadcasted from a room on the sixth floor of the building, with a view of the impressive roundabout and the centre monument. From their huge studio window, I could see that Monument Square still sat in perfect serenity, although rush hour was fast approaching. I took my seat in between what I could only assume were the producer and telephonist who also worked on the show. Ed Wank looked exactly as I imagined he would (probably because I'd seen a picture of him on the Internet). His bald head reflected the studio lights, and he sported a white T-shirt, jeans, and distinctive thick-framed glasses. Dave O'Brien, with whom I had exchanged e-mails, was the first of the two to greet me.

"Hiya, Richard. Thanks for coming. How are you finding Indianapolis?"

"Very clean, very nice. Purpose-built. Nice roundabout," I rambled.

Dave looked as if he had always been a cowboy and seemed to fit into the mode of country-and-western broadcaster very comfortably. He was even taller than me, at about six foot six, with greying dark hair, and he wore jeans, a loose, casual shirt, and a very country-and-western goatee with a connecting moustache. The banners and boards dotted around the studio bore the name Hank FM, so I couldn't for one minute forget where I was. It made me realize how un–country-and-western I must have looked, especially in the wake of Brad Cotter. Apart from riding a horse once when I was ten, and being subjected to the many John Denver singles in my dad's record collection, I wasn't exactly in the same league.

Over a Shania Twain hit and the obligatory advertisement

break, Dave made me feel totally at ease and engaged in idle small talk about my journey so far, while Ed used any gap in the broadcast available to him to promote their next guest.

"We have a real criminal in the studio with us, and he'll be coming up next."

By the time it was my turn to go on, I was relaxed and enjoyed every minute in the limelight, beginning with their opening question, a simple "How are you, Rich?" which I completely disregarded, going straight for the jugular.

"Your real name is Wank?" I asked. "You should have gone to a high school in England. You would have had the mickey really taken out of you with a surname like that!"

The interview must have lasted for about ten minutes (twenty with adverts and songs), and in that time I explained what had happened to me, regaling the hosts with tales of my previous exploits and telling them of the fun I'd had in Chicago with the police and fishing in my pyjamas. All of it went down well.

After I admitted I had eaten garlic whilst at the cinema the previous evening, hoping the cops wouldn't be waiting for me on the way out, the interview ended on a bizarre note about petrol and how outraged the Americans were for being made to pay over $2 for a gallon. I made them feel an equal measure of shock and relief after I revealed that the British pay over $6 a gallon.

"Thanks for popping in, Rich," remarked Dave as he began to fade in yet another hit.

"It's been a pleasure."

"And people can follow your progress on your Web site or something?" he added as the song's introduction was racing towards the lyrics.

I knew how radio worked—I had to get a last line in before the lyrics.

"They can follow our progress if they want, but they'd

have to do it in their own car!" Laughter followed, and we were faded out.

Although I hadn't expected to, I very much enjoyed our stopover in Indianapolis. It may not be the biggest or most exciting city in America, and with a nickname like "America's Crossroads," it's hardly the most picturesque. But the city's tramps were the friendliest and most courteous I'd ever met. If even the poorest, downtrodden vagrants of a city felt jolly and upbeat, then surely that spoke volumes for the overall mood of the city.

I wasn't 100 percent sure that the woman who appeared behind us was a tramp, as she made no attempt to ask for any money. But as we waited to cross the road I noticed that she had no shoes on her feet and her only possession seemed to be a small plastic bag hanging loosely from her right wrist, so I guessed she was.

"Whoa! Jesus!" she shouted as she stepped onto a large metal grid covering whatever lay beneath the sidewalk. Then she moved on to the next grid, bending over into a similar position as before and staring into the drop. "Whoa! Jesus!"

In Indianapolis, it seemed, every tramp had a gimmick or something different to offer to the general public. Shouting "Whoa! Jesus!" was obviously this woman's niche. After leaving her behind, we were instantly approached by a homeless man in charge of sports development, who taught me some basketball moves in exchange for a few cents. Indianapolis was fast becoming my favourite metropolis. By world terms the city was brand-new and didn't have much of a cultural feel to it. But it was a complete joy to simply amble the streets.

It wasn't long until another vagrant came to assist us. He kindly pointed us back in the direction of our motel even though I knew where it was, but it was a kind gesture, a sign of the city's overwhelming and unquestionable benevolence. As we thanked the gentleman and went on our way, he called us back to show us a handful of identical pictures of the city's capitol that had somehow come into his possession.

"Here, boys, have a postcard."

So nice.

12
PAIL ALE

We had only just arrived in St. Louis, a quick four hours from Indianapolis, but Bateman seemed to have just one thing in mind.

"Let's go to Hooters!"

"I'm not really that hungry right now, mate."

"Nor am I. I just wanna go to Hooters."

How could I refuse? I didn't want to disappoint Bateman, and if I had to keep him happy by paying another visit to the restaurant with waiteresses who wear small orange shorts and skin-hugging vests, I was willing to make the sacrifice.

Over a couple of beers, we discussed the reason for our being in St. Louis.

"So, what law is it today, then?" asked Bateman.

"It's illegal here to sit on a street curb whilst drinking beer out of a bucket. Don't know why."

"OK," replied Bateman, who seemed entirely at ease with the absurdity of it all.

St. Louis, it appeared, wasn't the only place to have such an odd decree. I could have broken this one in the Pullman area of Chicago if I had not been busy fishing in my pyjamas or evading cops in the world's slowest car chase ever.

My brand-new bucket cost me $1.04 (Missouri had a

lower sales tax rate than Utah, at 4.225 percent) in another local dollar shop. I rejoined Bateman in the car with a spring in my step, a bucket, and a single can of lager in my hand. I was ready.

St. Louis, home of blues and jazz music, and the birthplace of both T. S. Eliot and Chuck Berry, was founded by French fur trader Pierre Laclède in 1764. Since that time, the city has been under both French and Spanish rule. The mass immigration that St. Louis experienced when the Americans bought the state from the French seems to have disguised any visible link to its colonial past. And if the tramps were any indication as to how positively disposed the residents might be, we wouldn't be making any friends in St. Louis.

The road we selected to take us to the heart of the city took us through the roughest and poorest parts of St. Louis, where we were besieged by the local vagrants. Even when we stopped at a petrol station to buy fuel, a woman approached to ask for some money. Normally, you give some small change, receive a simple thank-you for your consideration, and leave with a sense of compassion. Things obviously worked slightly differently in St. Louis. The woman, who was hassling Bateman incessantly, didn't even look pleased when Bateman finally crumbled to the nagging and proffered two dollars after paying for the fuel.

"I gave her a couple of bucks and she asked for more!" he said when he returned to the car. "Cheeky bitch."

After parking the car by the riverfront—the Mississippi River separates St. Louis, Missouri, from East St. Louis in Illinois—we were confronted with the defining symbol of St. Louis . . . and another tramp. The 630-foot Gateway Arch is the largest structure in the city. It's basically a large piece of curved metal that couldn't look more out of place if it tried. Nevertheless, standing beneath the construction, in between the two stainless-steel bases and staring up at its apex, you experience a sense of wonder and can only marvel at the engineering of the arch. It is strangely beautiful, visually phenomenal, and absolutely pointless. And it cost $15 million back in 1963. Only a city that had once passed a law forbidding the drinking of lager out of a bucket could think to commission a multimillion-dollar arc for the sole purpose of symbolising the gateway to the American West.

We returned to the car after experiencing the arch, and I grabbed the bucket and can of lager. I made my way to a suitable sidewalk where a picture could be taken of me with the arch in the background. I wanted to prove I'd been in St. Louis and that no cheap chicanery had taken place. As we strolled down the street and back towards the arch, Bateman and I were stopped in the street by—yep, you've guessed it— another beggar. The gentleman, in jeans and a white T-shirt, paid no attention to the mix of strange objects I had in my possession and began to plead his case.

"Look, man," he began, "my mama's dead."

"I'm sorry to hear that," I replied.

"Yeah. I haven't eaten in like a week," he said as he lifted his shirt up, revealing a stomach that, I must admit, didn't seem too undernourished. "I was wondering if you had any money so I could get some food. You can't get anything in this city for under ten bucks."

Ten dollars! He wanted ten dollars?

"I don't have ten dollars, mate, but you can have all the change I've got." Just wanting to get on with the lawbreaking, I emptied my wallet and thrust what must have been more than a dollar into his hand. Bateman did the same. Unimpressed with the amount he had received, the man turned and simply walked away without a word.

"He didn't even thank us," Bateman yelled in disbelief.

"He didn't even give us a postcard either."

Finally, with no superfluous structures or ungrateful

tramps around to disturb me, I sat down on the curb and opened the can of lager. My previous experience working behind a bar proved no help at all in the pouring of the lager into the bucket, and so the contents consisted mostly of head. Just as I raised the plastic pail to my mouth, a car pulled up at the traffic light. Although the monolithic Gateway Arch stood directly in front of them, the people inside the car were clearly much more interested in me and what I was doing. For the briefest of moments, I was St. Louis's greatest tourist attraction—the idiot sitting on a curb drinking out of a bucket. I drank two mouthfuls, which I decided was enough. When I looked up at my audience again, I realised they weren't laughing at me but seemed to look on with pity and pathos. I should have asked for ten dollars. But the light suddenly turned to green and their brief witness to street crime came to an end as they pulled away and traveled into the distance.

As I wiped the lager from my lips, I calculated that we had now attempted to break thirteen laws, and achieved victories in eight of them. It was time for a celebration St. Louis style.

People had told me that before I left St. Louis I should experience one of the many jazz bars in the city. As we ventured south to find a suitable music venue, I thought it strange that in a city so famous for that type of music, the only things I noticed in the downtown area were banks, expensive hotels, and surly tramps, none of which seemed jazzy to me in the slightest. I can't say I had imagined Louis Armstrong lookalike contests or saxophonists playing on street corners, but nothing shouted out or even mildly whispered to me that this was a town famous for the blues.

At the southern end of Broadway, which sounded like a

fitting place to find jazz and blues clubs, we parked in a spot that was dark and gloomy, in part because of the freeway that ran above us. This part of Broadway, it seemed from the vast array of clubs, had to be the jazz capital of St. Louis, and the decision we were left with now was which one we should enter. The first we passed turned out to be the most expensive, and the empty seats and lack of audience kept us walking in search of a club that was bursting with energy. Then, like buses, two came along together, right opposite each other. They both had live bands, which appeared to be mandatory for such clubs, but there was an obvious winner: although the club across the road had an outdoor seating area with colourful paper lanterns like the deck of a river party boat, it was, after all, across the road and a full sixty yards away, and the club we were standing directly outside was falling distance away and had two empty seats at the bar.

BB's Jazz, Blues, and Soups, a nightspot that proudly boasts that the building has been used as a boardinghouse and "house of ill repute," was jam-packed, and it was completely understandable why the two vacant seats we had seen through the window had been quickly occupied by other patrons by the time Bateman and I finally arrived at the bar. We stood back from the bar with the many other people who had arrived too late for a seat, and we blended in quite well. As at other tourist attractions, all walks of life jostled shoulders as people attempted to squeeze their way through the packed space in search of one of the small tables in the centre of the bar, each with its own table light. The glow of the red lampshades and the smoky atmosphere reminded me of the villain's gentlemen's club in a James Bond movie. From what I could make out, there were going to be a dozen acts throughout the evening, and each one therefore was only allowed a strictly limited time onstage. As we drank our first round, a changeover took place and the MC welcomed Skeet Rodgers and the Inner City Blues Band (an unforgettable name due both to its length and to the fact that their adoring fans held a banner aloft throughout the thrilling performance). Bateman and I remained by the wall near the bar. Luckily, I could tower above the other standees to see if a table became available. As the band finished, everyone joined in with me by rising to their feet in a standing ovation; I applauded with them and whistled. Skeet Rodgers was definitely on fire, but I directed the bulk of my applause to the row of ladies who had held the banner so perfectly and admirably and whose arms must have been aching. A remarkable act of fan fortitude.

As Skeet and his posse left the stage to make room for the next act, I looked around the rest of the building for somewhere to sit. Rows of tables were huddled on what I assumed was normally the dance floor. The real jazz and blues fans (the ones who'd got there early enough to get a table) sat with friends and coworkers enjoying every minute of what was on show. Photo after photo of the music's legends adorned the walls of the club. B. B. King, Johnny Copeland, and James Cotton hung alongside popular jazz artists such as Louis Armstrong and Billie Holiday in a who's who gallery of the industry's iconic figures. It wasn't until I placed my beer on a table further up the wall that I noticed a particular space not dedicated to a jazz or blues star but aimed directly at me. The sign simply read:

Sec. 14-03-070
It is against city ordinances in any street, sidewalk, parking lot or alley to consume alcoholic beverages. This will result in a $500 fine or not more than 90 days in jail.

There was no mention of a bucket, but considering that just an hour ago I'd been drinking on the curb, the sign's appearance seemed just a tad too coincidental for my liking.

The next day, it was time for our short stay in St. Louis to come to an end. Neither of us was too upset. Saying goodbye to the city was a farewell to ungrateful tramps and laws that weren't terribly exciting to break. St. Louis made us reconsider whether we'd go to any more big cities soon. I genuinely enjoyed the smaller towns and meeting the people who lived there. Small-town America had characters full of obscurities and intrigue. Unfortunately, getting back to small-town America, or any other place for that matter, seemed to be a bit troublesome.

"Why isn't the bloody boot opening?" Bateman shouted while pressing the boot-lock button on the remote repeatedly.

"Has it run out of batteries?" I replied.

The electronic button that instantly opens the boot either was not operational or had no power. Either way, it refused to open. Bateman tried to unlock the doors instead.

"It doesn't even unlock it! What's going on?"

I took a step back and shrugged before I noticed the car's registration. Our other car's number plate I had learnt off by heart due to the number of times I was asked to write it when checking into motels; this one I hadn't but I was sure it was registered to the state of Michigan. This car wasn't. I turned around and approached Bateman, gently tapping him on the shoulder.

"Bateman, it's not our car. That's our one there," I said as I turned him around and pointed him to an identical car. Well, it wasn't exactly identical; this other car's boot was wide open.

Travelling south and crossing the Mississippi River for the third and final time, we entered the state of Tennessee, where I was hoping my brief encounter with a country-and-western star had me fully prepared for an aquatic version of a typical cowboy activity.

13
JAIL BAIT

Our first crossing of the Mississippi's mighty banks en route to Chicago signified to us that we had entered eastern America. This third crossing, into Tennessee, indicated our arrival in the South. As we pulled off the interstate and into a rest area, I popped in to the tourist information centre and looked around for a motel coupon guide, as I usually do when entering a new state. The coupon guides, aimed at tourists travelling through the country, are great not only for finding accommodation whilst travelling on interstates but also for saving a few bucks. As always, a heap of hundreds sat near the door, but I felt I had to continue through to the desk where the empty information centre's clerk stood, waiting expectantly for a conversation.

"Hi, I was just after one of these motel coupon things."

I would write her exact reply, but I didn't understand a word she said. We were very definitely in the South.

I did manage to understand Precious in the Tennessee Welcome Center in Memphis. With her help I was able to locate the closest state park that permitted fishing. It seemed I was destined for the town of Millington, just north of Memphis, and Meeman-Shelby State Park.

In the state of Tennessee it is illegal to catch a fish with a lasso. Actually, it's also illegal to catch a fish with your bare hands in Kansas, but I thought that might be raising the bar a little too high. So Tennessee's obscure angling decree got the nod. I had already savoured the sweet taste of success in my previous two aquatic endeavours, spear hunting in Utah and fishing in my pyjamas in Chicago, so I felt pretty confident. I did have some concern over the wording of the law. In Chicago I only had to fish, so simply holding the rod proved adequate. Utah merely required I have the prerequisite mind-set of hunting for a whale, regardless of whether the beast was slain or not. This was the first time I would have to actually catch the animal in order for the law to be broken. Success was not guaranteed, and I knew it would be virtually impossible if I attempted to lasso the fish in the traditional way. It was time to do some creative thinking and go to a hardware store for supplies.

Obviously rope was a necessity. A store employee kindly showed me the way to the appropriate aisle, but the enormous selection of rope on offer was incomprehensible. I never knew different types of rope had names. It was like visiting a Starbucks and being offered everything from an Arabian Mocha Sanani to a Columbian Narino Supremo when all you want is a cup of coffee. I did have a look for "lasso rope" to see if such a thing existed. It didn't. I settled for a 20-foot length whose technical name I don't know, but which I called "a pretty thick piece of white rope." Luckily Millington had the ubiquitous Wal-Mart just down the road from the hardware store, and it was about to be called upon for a second time to find the materials for a cheap but effective piece of fishing equipment.

The discovery of an Eagle Claw Catfish Outfit completed my search. The set included, among other fishing equipment, floats, weights, and a selection of hooks. Off we went to Meeman-Shelby State Park, where we would tackle law fourteen.

The road to the park took us through such towns such as Cuba and Locke, and since we were down south, the road appeared to be lined with more churches than houses. With it being a Wednesday, entrance to the park was free, as it is on that particular day every week. Not that it would have mattered. There was no toll box or barrier gate; instead the system of payment was simple and honesty-based. Any other day of the week you would pay the $3 tariff and take one of the park's rear-mirror hangers, which lay on top of the honesty box and could be taken for free anyway. Not that I would ever dream of doing such a thing—I'm not one to break the law.

The whole park seemed deserted. When I arrived at the visitors' centre to pick up a map of the area there was little sign of staff, let alone visitors. The map identified Poplar Tree Lake as the biggest and most popular fishing spot. It had a pier, some sort of museum, and a boat hire centre. It sounded ideal.

In reality Poplar Tree Lake wasn't the most idyllic of fishing hot spots. The pier turned out to be a small wooden jetty that protruded a short distance into the brown and murky-looking water of the lake, the museum was a display of stuffed wild animals, and the boat hire centre (which was a circular hut) was shut for lunch and not due to reopen for another three-quarters of an hour. The lake itself was vast and deserted. If anyone frequented the state park at this time of year, they didn't seem to come to Poplar. Our car was only one of three vehicles in the car park, one of which must have belonged to the lone woman who stood on the pier fishing.

Although the temperature had climbed back above a hundred for the first time since Arizona, I was determined to make this law a fourth victory in a row—unprecedented! I removed all the materials from the boot of the car to construct my lasso.

I was obviously never going to catch a fish using the traditional lassoing technique of spin, throw, land, and tighten—I knew from my research that even if I could throw the rope, it wouldn't penetrate the water. Not even a trained lasso artist could do that. I had a cleverer scheme, though, oh yes. Tying the end of the rope to itself and creating a lasso, I then tied catgut line to the noose of the rope and attached the hook. The bait supplied in the box kit looked similar to an Oxo cube and reeked of something unimaginable that only fish could be stupid enough to taste. I put the disgusting thing on the hook and my lasso was complete.

With thirty minutes still remaining until we could hire a boat, we decided to try our hand at fishing from the banks and attempted this from under a nearby tree so we could shelter from the heat of the day. Within a minute of my maiden cast, the line was quickly tangled up in the roots by the shore and I managed to lose my hook, my bait, and, with them, my dignity. God, this was going to be difficult. Why on earth was this a law, anyway? To my mind, the men or women who managed to catch a fish with a lasso should be held in esteem, not in custody. In a way it's a similar achievement to streaking at a sports event: you know what you've done is admirable and courageous and what you've achieved will be talked about for years, but at the end of it all you will be arrested.

"I think we're going to have to hire a boat, mate," I told Bateman.

At precisely one o'clock we returned to the hire centre. Although the water seemed too dirty for any kind of life to survive, the many pictures posted on the hut of fishermen holding outstanding bass and other varieties of fish from bream to catfish seemed to suggest I was wrong.

Ten minutes later a pickup truck entered the car park and the owner made his way towards his hut. The gentleman, sporting jeans and a brown T-shirt with TENNESSEE emblazoned on the chest, in case I'd forgotten where I was, looked warily at me as if I were his first customer in a very long time. Looking around the lake and at the hire book, I figured I probably was.

"Hiya. I'd like to hire a boat for the afternoon, please."

"Just the two of you, is it?"

"It is."

"Can you sign here, please?"

As I signed the standard disclaimer, which put all legal responsibility onto my shoulders in the event that I died, I noticed that I required a fishing permit. They cost only $3 but were purchasable only from the local shop, over five miles away down single-lane woodland roads. I couldn't afford to waste precious time for that.

"You gonna go fishing?" he asked.

"Well, we don't have any rods." I didn't want to lie to him.

"OK, then. That'll be eight dollars for the boat, please."

Our vessel, a tatty-looking but robust rowing boat, had no engine and only two oars. This didn't upset either of us. Apart from the fact that it was hard work in the heat to move both us and the boat, we moved faster than we ever had when we were powered by the 13-horsepower engine across Jordanelle in Utah.

In what seemed no time at all we had travelled about 300 yards and manoeuvred into a small inlet on the other side of the lake. Here we could fish away from the prying eyes of the boat hire man. The inlet was no more than 100 yards long by 30 yards wide, and the shade made the water look an even darker shade of brown than the rest of the lake. Dropping my line into the water, we began to paddle furiously to wherever we saw bubbles emerge on the surface, taking that as a sure sign of marine life—or else a sign that the scorching temperature had begun to boil the lake's water.

We decided to paddle towards the shade under the assumption that the fish would also prefer the shade on a blisteringly warm summer's day. Unfortunately, as we manoeuvred the boat towards the end of the lake and the trees, my line snagged on a tree branch that lay just beneath the surface, and I lost my bait for the second time that afternoon. I reapplied a fresh piece of bait, releasing the putrid smell once more as Bateman and I removed our T-shirts in an effort to combat the heat. All we could do now was wait.

"I spy with my little eye something beginning with *T*," Bateman stated.

"Tree?"

"Yep."

"Right, my turn. I spy with my little eye something beginning with . . ." I had to make this one tricky to pass the time. "*M*."

"Mud," Bateman answered instantly.

"Yeah. That was quick."

I looked around. The problem with this game was all that was surrounding us was water, trees, mud, insects, and the boat. As far as the variety of options for a successful game of I Spy went, we were hardly spoilt for choice. At least the game had passed a minute or so—enough time for a fish to become attached to my line. I pulled my lasso out of the water to discover there was no fish attached. But, surprisingly, the bait remained on the hook. As I dropped my line into the water in hope once more, the sound of a woodpecker emanated from the trees behind us, bringing with it a glimmer of hope for a different game.

"I hear with my little ear something beginning with *W*," I said with a smile on my face, evidently looking as if I was enjoying the entire experience. Bateman simply glared back at me in a you-brought-me-here-and-now-you're-trying-to-make-me-play-this-stupid-game kind of way.

"Never mind, then. Shall we change location?"

"What's the point? We're not going to catch anything."

Bateman's confidence was somewhat lacking—probably because he had set up his own line and was losing bait as regularly as I was. I suppose the temperature, sweat, lack of success, and the fact we were 5,000 miles from home floating in a lake in Tennessee for no other reason than to catch a fish with a lasso must have gotten to him.

"Just use a net," he remarked.

"What?"

"Just use a net to catch the fish and I'll take a picture of you. No one will know the lasso wasn't used."

"Bateman. Bateman, Bateman, Bateman," I said. "I can't cheat. If I do, it would mean that our whole purpose for being out here was corrupt. There would be no rules anymore, and if the world had no rules it would descend into chaos."

"I've heard that line somewhere before," Bateman replied.

"Have you? I just made it up, I think."

By now more than an hour had passed and we had found another inlet on the other side of the lake that looked promising but, sadly, had no shade. I hadn't cheated and our little world remained on its fragile precipice, saved from falling into bedlam through the wrongful use of a net. Then, out of nowhere, just as my faith was being seriously tested, the most unexpected event occurred. I felt a gentle tug at the end of my line. I quickly wiped the sweat off my forehead, lifted my flip-flop off the excess rope, and gripped the line with my hand. This was it. I pulled and tugged at the rope and after a titanic struggle finally got my first look at the giant branch on which my line had snared.

"Shit! Let's just go back. This isn't getting us anywhere," I yelled as I threw my line back into the water in frustration.

It was definitely time to go. The sun had reached its peak by now, and Bateman and I knew in our hearts that this law was doomed.

As we made our way back to the small wooden harbour where the rest of the six or seven rowing boats lay, I happened to catch a quick look at the woman who'd been our only fishing companion. I could clearly see her pack up her belongings and leave her position by the lake completely emptyhanded with the exception of her rod and flask. If she couldn't catch anything with a rod, what chance did I have with a lasso?

We got back in the car and continued south, towards Memphis and into Mississippi. My new coupon book advised that the little frontier town of Horn Lake offered "comfortable and affordable" accommodation. With a name like that, there was only one place Bateman wanted to eat.

"Let's go to Hooters!"

"Bateman, just because the name of the town is Horn Lake doesn't mean it'll have a Hooters. It's only a small town."

By early evening we found ourselves propped up at the bar of Hooters of Horn Lake being served by a waitress garbed in the unvarying Hooters uniform. Cassandra, who had left Texas to work in Horn Lake, was studying to be a nurse but could have easily been a model, and her scanty Hooters attire, I'm pleased to say, left nothing to the imagination. Our newest friend must have been about twenty-one years of age, had long blond hair, and proved true the theory that blond hair correlates with a certain type of intellect when she took a sudden liking to our driving licences, which we had produced to purchase our drinks.

"Wow, they're pink. And what's this mean? Ours are nothing like these."

Whether it was our untenable charm, ravishing good looks, or Bateman's promise to talk her through the history of the ancient symbolisations of the DVLA (Driving and Vehicle Licensing Agency), over the course of our two-hour drinking session we had managed to secure a night on the town with Cassandra and her friend after she finished work.

"I'll pick you up around eleven at your motel, OK?"

"OK," we replied excitedly in unison.

As our motel television, turned to CNN, informed us that Hurricane Irene would arrive in North Carolina in a matter of days (just about when we were due to arrive, in fact), we busily decided what to wear and wondered if Cassandra was even going to appear. Maybe she had just invited us out so we would stop talking to her and leave the restaurant, and we had taken the bait, unlike the numerous fish that supposedly lived in Poplar Tree Lake. As Bateman spruced himself up and tried to find clothes that would best suit the environment of a club, I kept reminding him that it was all a big waste of time and that Cassandra was never going to turn up. Just then the phone rang.

"She's outside!"

I can't say I remember much about the club, and the extra cans of lager we'd downed before the phone rang certainly didn't aid my already failing memory. The club was definitely in Memphis, and I recall it took us about fifteen minutes to get there from the lobby of our motel. The club was not the biggest I've ever been to and had a live band playing instead of the usual head-thumping repetitive beat I usually associate with dance clubs. Cassandra's friend was a young girl named Hope, who had medium-length black hair and I would guess was somewhere in her early twenties. Both girls were excellent company and I was glad that now, away from the environment of Hooters, where Cassandra's job was to be pleasant to us, the girls were themselves and great people to be around. Every round Bateman bought came to over $30, and I remember that when I purchased the same it came to under $20. Goodness knows what Bateman was buying extra.

I must admit, I don't remember my actions in the club that night, but we hadn't arrived until just before midnight, so I couldn't have had much time to embarrass myself. We were sitting at a table near the dance floor, and as I looked across at Bateman and Cassandra, who were chatting away quite merrily, I realized my attention that evening was supposed to be directed towards Hope.

After far too many rounds, the house lights of the club rose and we left the premises, walking back across the road and into the car. Although we'd all had a bit to drink, Cassandra was adamant that she'd been closely monitoring her alcohol consumption and was perfectly capable of driving us back to the Mississippi border and Horn Lake. We were too drunk to think about it much. I must have had a few minutes of sleep on our return to the motel, because before I knew it, we had stopped in a shop's parking space just yards from our motel. I assumed Bateman was buying cigarettes. As he left the shop, I saw him do a double take at the car.

"Come look at this, Rich."

Thinking Cassandra must have some sort of roadkill jammed in the grille of her car, I leapt out and joined Bateman at the front. There was no cat spread across the car's tyre, no deer leg hanging out of the grille; not even a fly had smeared the windscreen.

"Look at the car," Bateman demanded.

Then it hit me (not the car). Even the staggering amount of alcohol I had consumed that night could not alleviate the shock I felt as I surveyed the car's body. I felt instantly sober again. All holiday I'd been careful and constantly aware. Yet when my defences were down, when drink had lowered my guard, I had allowed stupidity to breach my rational resistance: I had accepted a lift back to my motel with two girls I barely knew who were probably in no fit state to drive a car that was a positively unmistakable shade of red.

"It's red, Rich. The car's red."

"Yes, I can see that, Bateman. I think I'll walk the last few yards to the motel."

The girls joined us back in our room, and Bateman took great joy in impressing them by leaping off his bed and crashing down onto mine so we could all laugh at the ridiculous position he landed in. This continued for about ten minutes until Cassandra asked what her car had to do with my funny reaction five minutes earlier—and simultaneously the leg of my bed broke.

"What's so weird about my car being red?" she asked. After Bateman explained, Cassandra sat down on the edge of Bateman's unbroken bed, clearly ruffled by the story.

"Wow, that's weird. My god, that's spooky. I could have been killed or something."

"No, *I'm* the one who was to be killed," I added, trying to aid the situation.

"But I could have killed you. My car is red." Cassandra was quite obviously one of those girls who read horoscopes and believed every word.

"It doesn't matter. Look, nothing happened to me. I'm fine. That woman was just talking rubbish," I added. Cassandra shook her head and stared at the ground.

"Bateman, just show her your driving licence. That'll cheer her up."

I'm not sure if he ever did produce his licence to raise her morale, but if so, he did it in the dark, as the two disap-

peared beneath the covers of his bed, leaving Hope and me
to do the same. I couldn't stop one thought from continually
racing through my mind—why couldn't I have met Hope in
San Francisco?

Checkout times are always cruel in motels, especially when
you don't get to sleep until well after the sunrise. The rather
enjoyable evening and the (still) living evidence that the
crackpot in Long Beach was indeed just that soothed any
disappointment regarding our failed Tennessee fishing expe-
dition. Brenda's premonition that some person was going to
offer me a lift in a red car might have come true, but her foreboding was clearly misplaced. As Hope and her friend left in
Cassandra's car, which in the morning light gleamed a fantastic shade of scarlet, Bateman and I returned to our own
car to drive towards another one of the psychic's forewarn-
ings. She had envisioned a court case in my future. Well, we
were about to travel south to Oxford, Mississippi, where I
hoped I would be seeing the front and back of a courthouse
more than a hundred times. As we closed our doors and
made our way back to the interstate, I looked at Bateman
with a big smirk on my face.

"See, you were wrong. You thought I was going to die if I
got into a red car. That woman said danger lurked, and the
result was the exact opposite, really. I'm absolutely fine," I
boasted proudly.

Bateman turned in his seat and stared into my eyes
intensely.

"You don't know that. You could have caught something."

14

IT'S LEFT, LEFT, AND LEFT AGAIN

Ever since the fateful Balderdash game at Christmas and the extensive research that followed, I couldn't wait to reach Oxford, Mississippi. The town was home to my favourite of all the laws I was in America to break—in Oxford it is illegal to drive around the town square more than a hundred times in a single session. Brilliance, sheer brilliance.

As we made our way into the centre of the town, the leafy neighbourhoods gave way to a sudden avenue of shops that culminated at the foot of the county courthouse, present-ing a T-junction at which I could only turn right. I'd seen the courthouse before during my Internet research about the town and recognised it instantly.

"This is it, Bateman."

There, standing in front of me, was the Lafayette County courthouse, which was the centrepiece of the town square. The rectangular white building, with its mighty Doric white pillars and pristine European-style clock tower, stood be-hind a statue which made a superb start and finishing line to the Oxford Grand Prix. Although I didn't plan to break the law until later on in the evening, I got a good idea of what to expect, as it took Bateman and me four laps to find a vacant parking space.

Oxford was named after the English city as part of an ultimately successful campaign to persuade the University of Mississippi to locate its main campus in the town. Ole Miss, as the university is more commonly known, now enrolls more than 11,000 students, and during term time, when the students descend onto this affluent town in what is otherwise a poor area, the population nearly doubles. In mid-August, the 12,000-plus permanent residents, Bateman, and I were free to explore the town in almost perfect peace. I was excited to learn that William Faulkner had grown up in the town after moving from nearby New Albany when he was five. Sadly, my excitement was short-lived when I realized I had confused the author of classics such as *The Sound and the Fury* and *As I Lay Dying* with the actor who played Columbo, Peter Falk. The statue of the man, which sits on a bench outside City Hall, was not of a cigar-wielding man in a trench coat asking for "just one more thing."

The shops surrounding the square are archetypal of small-town America, and the topiary gardens that straddle the sidewalks and encircle lampposts make the exploration of the town a thoroughly enjoyable one. The town boasts antiques shops, bookstores with upstairs cafés, and Neilson's, a department store almost unchanged since 1897, delightful assets to a town where quaintness seems almost overemphasised. These pleasing if incongruous winding streets and the bizarre features such as the old-fashioned English telephone box in the northeast corner of the square (dedicated by John and Laura Valentine from Oxfordshire, as the plaque informed us) are not enough to disguise the town's shameful past.

In 1962, Oxford was the site of one of the most brutal displays of racial hatred ever witnessed in the state. When James Meredith was allowed to enroll as the first black student at Ole Miss after eighteen months of legal and political wrangling, the decision caused fury, resulting in a riot on

Meredith's first day after he was smuggled in by federal troops. The riot, in which bottles and rocks were thrown at the military personnel, left 3 people dead and 160 injured. Despite constant threats, Meredith graduated a year later and as a defiant gesture wore a "Never" badge (the segregationist slogan of Governor Ross Barnett) upside down. Maybe it was because of the riots that the law about driving in the town square existed, or maybe it had been implemented much earlier. This was the one law I definitely wanted to know more about. It just seemed too strange that such a law would have been passed. Surely people could drive around the square any number of times they wished—or were they under constant scrutiny by the police, who had been counting since the car had entered the square and were waiting for the conclusion of the 101st lap? With no library visible in which to conduct my research, I visited a resplendent bookshop by the name of Square Books, just opposite the start-finish line and whose upstairs café would act as a perfect grandstand for the proceedings later on that day. The shopkeeper informed me that the town was home to two libraries, the superior facility being located on the university campus, less than a mile from the square.

With students having grabbed their backpacks and jumped on trains around Europe or booked into grotty hostels in any number of countries and the academic year not restarting for another eight weeks, the campus was very quiet. I painstakingly climbed the library's steps, explained to the woman at the front desk why I had come thousands of miles from home, and requested her assistance for the most ridiculous of reasons. She directed me downstairs, where someone would be able to help. From there I was sent to the upper level of the building, back down to the ground level once more, and then to the other side of the room, where, after my fourth embarrassing explanation, I was told to go to the law library, on the other side of the campus.

"Stuff this; I'm going to wait in the car," Bateman said. I think he had the right idea.

Behind the front desk of the law library sat the only person, other than me, in the entire building. After disturbing the man, who probably wasn't used to having to talk to people, I asked if he knew anything of the origin of the law or if he was aware if it was still in force today. He shrugged, laughed, and presented me with the Oxford, Mississippi, city ordinance book.

"If it is, it'll be in here."

I spent thirty minutes searching the thousand-page file for the law, but after reading the pages that covered the sections on traffic, peaceful protest, automobiles, and miscellaneous, I ran out of ideas on where it might be. If it did exist, it was well hidden somewhere in the other 900-odd pages. Even if I had found the law, I knew the wording would give me no clue as to the law's origin or background.

Still, Crombie's book said it was law, and as that was my guide, I planned to go forward with the criminal endeavour. I joined Bateman back at the car, and we agreed that we would begin the laps at seven that evening, after we had returned to our motel and slept off our hangovers.

I never did get any sleep that afternoon, instead creating a tally chart and checklist on which Bateman could record the laps and any events of interest that occurred. By six o'clock we had made our way to the town square with a full tank of gas.

The course was a simple one. It wouldn't inspire the NASCAR organisers to relocate the Indy 500, nor was it in the same league as Brands Hatch or Le Mans, but it was a track where I had reserved pole position and on which I would definitely not be lapped. It did have pedestrians to be wary of and wasn't as square as the name suggested. Oxford's pseudo–Grand Prix track wasn't even rectangular in shape and actually consisted of six mini straights in an obscure hexagonal design—unfortunately disqualifying it from being featured on *America's Greatest Roundabouts*. Luckily, the square was devoid of any sort of traffic lights or traffic calming systems, so laps could be completed with relative ease. The statue, I'd seen earlier, which was of some Confederate figure, was selected as my start line and was near a pedestrian crossing that led over to the bookshop I had visited earlier. Three other similar crossings were on the east, north, and west sides of the square. After the first corner, an easy left made its way to the rear of the courthouse, and the track widened to allow for the flow of added traffic from streets funneling into the square. There, the longest of the pedestrian crossings was to be found, and then the track made its way back to Van Buren Avenue, where the start-finish line stood.

Traffic lights would have been nice for the start of the event, but in their absence we thought we could make do with a woman who had positioned herself with an easel by her side, painting a picture of the scene south of the courthouse. I was hoping she was drawing a chequered flag to present to us for whenever we crossed the line after completing lap 101, but I didn't have time to tell her about my attempt before Bateman began the stopwatch on his mobile phone to begin the first of the laps.

From a standing start, I didn't expect a great deal from lap one, but it would be a good benchmark from which to calculate an average time for each of the following circuits. With a couple of cars joining me on "telephone turn," which stood on the rear of the courthouse and where the two other roads widened the track, I completed my virgin lap with a respectable time of 32 seconds. Lap two, without the hindrance of a standing start, was obviously going to be much quicker, and even with the interference of a pedestrian crossing the street I made it in under half a minute. It wasn't until lap twelve, when I recorded the fastest lap so far, that I felt as if breaking the law wouldn't take as long as I had once thought: it was the first lap without any interruptions of any nature, and it resulted in a course record: 25 seconds. Only eight laps later, disaster struck: two cars joining the square held me up, and then an entire family crossed the street, further delaying my progress to the line on a lap that took forty seconds to complete.

Lap thirty brought about a new fastest lap (24 seconds) and the departure of the woman and her easel from the statue, the woman taking one final look at the car she must have seen over twenty times—and surely must have featured in her painting as a permanent fixture of the town centre's scenic landscape.

By lap thirty-four, the course was beginning to become a tad repetitive, so I began to take a closer look at the buildings on the course. "Telephone turn" was home to First Bank and the city hall. Then I passed such noticeable landmarks as a pub with upper decking for a perfect view of my progress, and Duvall's, now a clothing store but the first location of the First National Bank of Oxford, founded by Faulkner's grandfather. It's probably because of my interest in my surroundings and my lack of attention to pedestrians and other hazards that the lap ended with a new fastest lap time of 23 seconds—a record that would stand for the remainder of the day. I was back in the mood for speed, but the following lap was ruined by the presence of a barrage of pedestrians. I also briefly saw a few police officers, but none was wearing a bulletproof vest, and they took no obvious exception to our flag.

It wasn't until lap fifty-two until the presence of the law was felt once more, but that time the cops quickly turned down Van Buren Avenue. I was free to complete the remaining forty-eight laps without fear of a police stop.

This was the only time on my trip the lawbreaking was somewhat dull. I had anticipated this happening, and the timing of the laps was a vain attempt to thwart boredom. Fast laps were now few and far between, and after recording times of 28, 29, and even 32 seconds, I was beginning to wonder just how many lives I had endangered to produce the record lap time. Bateman, who by now had resigned himself to the all-important job of tallying up the laps and frequently reminding me of just how many remained, sat quietly in the passenger seat, hoping something more interesting would happen. He was probably paying close attention to the passing business hoping to catch a glimpse of a Hooters he had not spotted on the previous laps.

After sixty laps, I half expected to have some sort of fan base who knew what we were doing or at least noticed that we had passed them dozens of times and would maybe wave each time I went by. Ever since the lady and her easel had left the square, not a single person seemed to have noticed that we had passed them several times. It wasn't until lap eighty-two that a couple on a bench to the east of the courthouse opposite the pedestrian crossing appeared to notice our frequent appearances. The constant puzzled looks and pointing to our car, plus their change of posture—they'd been facing each other, evidently involved in a deep and meaningful discussion, but now had turned their bodies towards the road—made me feel as if we now dominated their conversation: "Louise, I love you and I've never felt this way about anyone in my life. We've been together now for over six years, and I've finally plucked up the courage to do this. I have one very important question to ask you. Louise . . . is it me or has that car passed us more than ten times already?" OK, maybe it wasn't as important as that, but you never know.

As far as they were aware, the two madmen who had driven past them had done so more than a dozen times. Little did they know that these madmen were well on their way to their ninetieth revolution. And we were hardly the most discreet or inconspicuous. I'm willing to bet that not only in Oxford or Mississippi but even in the entire continent of North America or maybe even the world, on that day we were the only drivers of a blue Dodge Neon with Cornish and British flags on the car's antenna and a flag of St. Piran displayed on the parcel shelf.

Sadly, the last laps didn't produce any records, and with a final lap time of 32 seconds, we crossed the finish line without the waving of a chequered flag or a presentation of champagne. Even the couple who were perplexed by our actions must not have been overly keen to know just why we had done what we did, as they quickly left the town square walking in the opposite direction from our parked car.

The total time for all 101 laps and therefore the completion of the entire lawbreaking episode was timed at 52 minutes and 19 seconds. That, for the statisticians amongst us and purely just for the record, resulted in an average lap time of 31.08 seconds. The most important datum to me was the fact that after failure in Tennessee, the drive was the fifteenth law I had attempted to break and the ninth in which I was victorious. That itself was a reason to celebrate, and although I wasn't planning on shaking up the entire contents of a gigantic bottle of bubbly as though I were standing on a Formula One podium, at least there was a bar we could enjoy a small tipple in.

15
WATERY GRAVES

For only the third time in the holiday I awoke early enough the morning after the epic Grand Prix to experience the culinary delights of the motel's continental breakfast. As always, the choice of what to eat consisted of the usual bagels, apples, and fine array of breakfast cereals, but on this occasion I entered alone, as Bateman had taken to referring to the spread as "continental shit."

This was the first time I had eaten with no other guests around me. I had enjoyed meeting and conversing with Joye's Honduran mother in Phoenix and had had a delightfully peculiar encounter after my appearance on the *Wank and O'Brien Show* with a family from Surrey who had travelled down from Canada and had stayed overnight in Indianapolis in order to attend a folk music festival in Ohio. But in Oxford, not a soul wanted to hear my lap-by-lap commentary of what had occurred the previous evening. I was left on my own to wait for my bagel to pop out of the toaster. Unbelievable.

Finishing my bagel, I was then left with the tricky decision of which beverage to wash it all down with. I opted for the milk, stored in an industrial-sized container. Lowering my cup and holding it in place beneath the tap, I pulled lightly on the handle until a sufficient amount had been dispensed. I noticed that the flow of milk continued for several seconds after I had returned the handle to its original position. As I stepped away from the machine, still watching the dribble, the dispenser's handle fell off, and milk began gushing out. Shit.

I raced over to try to stanch the flow, but soon it had easily soaked my shorts and T-shirt and was now beginning to pour onto the floor. Not wanting to act cowardly (or get caught for it, as I was the only person in the dining room and would definitely suffer the blame), I couldn't simply run away from the danger zone, leaving whoever entered the breakfast room after my departure with a titanic struggle against a strong current of pasteurised milk in order to get to their morning bagel. I quickly grabbed the handle and did what any decent citizen would do—I placed the metal lever back over the tubing so delicately that whoever used it next was guaranteed to restart the torrential flow of white liquid and consider themselves the guilty party. (Well, it worked when I was younger.) No sooner had the handle been exquisitely and precisely positioned into place with only the smallest of drops emanating from the tap, when the torrent dramatically sprang back to life once again, saturating the carpet before I managed to pinch the tubing shut with my fingers. Now I was faced with a dilemma. Should I keep hold of the tubing until someone appeared (bearing in mind that I hadn't seen anyone since I woke up that morning) or run out of the room like a coward, leaving the container to empty its load and turn the breakfast room into a reservoir of milk? Luckily my decision was made easier by the appearance of one of the motel's cleaners.

"Excuse me, I could do with a bit of a hand here. I've kind of broken the handle of the milk container. I tried to fix it." The cleaner looked at the floor, the handle, and the four bowls of milk positioned on a drenched work surface and surrounded by cornflakes, which I had used in an earlier attempt to contain the milkfall, but said nothing.

"Um . . . but I couldn't," I added, as if the state of the room wasn't sufficient evidence.

The cleaner came over and took over the task of keeping the tube pinched shut. "Just go and contact the manager for me, will you?" he said.

I was only too glad to go find him and break the rather disturbing milk-related news.

Back on the road, having changed my shorts, it was time to concentrate on our next destination. Because of the simple fact that the interstate that would have taken us to Birmingham, Alabama, was still under construction, constant detours took Bateman and me through small-town Alabama, where the turns had such wonderful names as Natural Bridge and Brilliant. Thinking a detour might improve my chances of breaking another strange law, I flicked straight to Alabama in my book of laws and made quite an interesting discovery.

"Hey, Bateman, did you know that in an attempt to cut down on the number of laws that governed them, the residents of Brooksville, Alabama, applied to be governed by no other laws than the Ten Commandments?"

"Really? What *are* the Ten Commandments, anyway?" he replied.

"Um, 'Thou shall not steal . . .' "

"Murder?"

"Yeah, 'Thou shall not kill.' And 'Thou shall not have any other God but me,' or something like that. Adultery, keep the Sabbath day holy, and five others."

"They're in the Bible, aren't they?" asked Bateman

"Yeah, Old Testament, I think,"

"We'll look them up in one of those Gideons Bibles we always find in our motel when we get one."

"Yeah, sure. At least it can't spray me with milk."

For a second, I thought that trying to come up with the five remaining commandments would supply enough incentive for the start of another of our own specially devised travel games. That was until Bateman spotted the remains of a racoon that had somehow managed to impale itself on the raised cornerstone of the sidewalk in the town of Carbon Hill, where, not surprisingly, the scuba centre, 200 miles from the coast, had only recently closed down.

As the sun began to fall in the sky, it was obvious we were going to have to spend the night in the state of Georgia, a few hundred miles short of our next destination of Spartanburg, South Carolina. The decision to stay overnight in Atlanta was precipitated by the weather, which was rapidly deteriorating: suddenly the heavy rain striking the windscreen was more than the wipers could deal with. Following articulated lorries was a death trap, but passing them became impossible due to the zero visibility. The horrific driving conditions continued for well over an hour; by then the road was submerged under several inches of water in places, reminding me both of the severe storms we had fallen victim to in Globe and my dreaded milk incident earlier in the day. I began to wonder whether this was divine revenge for our blasphemy and/or lack of knowledge of the Ten Commandments. Thankfully, we managed to make it to a motel at the top of a hill (just in case), and the second after Bateman left to find somewhere to drink and I turned the television on, lightning knocked out the TV signal, leaving me with a screen that resembled the clarity of our windscreen during the severest part of the storm. As I lay on my bed with curtain ajar I could see that the lightning was beginning to become very frequent, striking almost like clockwork every three or four seconds. Through the slight gap in the curtains, the flashes were sharp and luminous against the night sky, and I couldn't help opening the door of the room to properly witness such a sight. I stood at the top of the outdoor stairs and waited for the next strike of atmospheric electricity. Surprisingly, it never arrived. As I turned back towards my room, wondering how the lightning that had been so frequent could simply stop, I then noticed that above the window of my room was a faulty light that flickered on and off incessantly. No lightning.

Thinking my chance of entertainment that evening had vanished, I decided to use the laptop Bateman had bought in Salt Lake City to check my e-mail. Sitting in my inbox was an e-mail from Dave O'Brien, who had replied to the message I'd sent him thanking him for inviting us onto his show. The most interesting part of his e-mail was the revelation that Bateman had sent Dave his own message, leaving his e-mail address in the hope that the intern who had first greeted us (whose name he had forgotten) would reply. Bateman planned to spend an additional two weeks in America after I flew home, and therefore I felt it was up to me, being the kindhearted friend that I am, to create a fake e-mail address for the girl and attempt to make him fly back to Indianapolis to see someone who didn't exist. Indianaradio girl@hotmail.com was plucked from thin air, and Angela was now known as "Lisa Jennings." Any doubts in my mind that this was a cruel trick to play on my friend were quickly eliminated when I e-mailed Dave about what I was doing and he replied that it was the "funniest thing he'd heard all day." With the e-mail sent to Bateman, purportedly from the girl, asking why he wanted her to get in touch, I left the room and went in search of my friend. It didn't take long. By this stage of the holiday Bateman had developed a sixth sense that could lead him quite effortlessly to the nearest Hooters.

I hadn't shaved for over a week, and the next morning I began to shave only the stubble that had grown on my cheeks and the top of my neck, leaving the facial hair on my chin and upper lip. In just under two weeks Bateman and I would be arriving in Boston, Massachusetts—a state where goatees were strictly forbidden.

Arriving in Spartanburg, we stopped for the first—and thankfully last—time on the holiday at McDonald's. We couldn't order right away, though, because Skyy, the cashier, found Bateman's accent hilarious.

"I love your accent. What's your name?" she asked in a deep southern drawl.

"Luke."

"Say it again."

"Luke."

"Hang on, one second." Skyy left her position behind the till and returned seconds later, dragging a male colleague by the collar. "Listen to this man say his name. Say it again."

"Luke."

"Isn't that so funny?" asked Skyy, holding her sides in laughter. She turned to her colleague in expectance of agreement.

"Don't worry, she's on drugs," he remarked with a straight face, and took Bateman's order. I had no reason not to believe him.

If any corporation were to sponsor this crime spree, I would imagine it would have to be Wal-Mart, because whenever I needed some sort of apparatus to aid me in my illicit adventures, the superstore always came up trumps. Wal-Mart in Spartanburg was certainly no exception, and following our shopping trip, Bateman and I left in search of Magnolia Cemetery, armed with a slice of watermelon. It's illegal to eat a watermelon in the cemetery, and not only in Spartanburg. Other than laws that prohibit spitting on sidewalks and the carrying of ice cream cones in your back pocket, laws pertaining to the eating of a watermelon in a specific area are by far the most common across states all over America. Beech Grove, Indiana, for instance, has a similar decree.

Spartanburg, with a population that exceeded forty thousand, was by no means a small town. It was a Sunday, and so there was no tourist information kiosk or Chamber of Commerce open to help us find our way to the cemetery. I took a nervous bite out of the melon.

Hoping that Magnolia Cemetery was located on Magnolia Street, we drove around Spartanburg in the hope that sooner or later we would come across either the cemetery or the correct street. From the interstate, we joined Route 26, which delivered us to West Main Street. From there, the roads in the centre of town forced us to turn north onto Daniel Morgan Avenue, where Liberty Street joined Magnolia Street.

Cutting our speed, Bateman and I kept our eyes peeled for any area that resembled a graveyard in any way. After crossing a railroad track, Magnolia Street passed Johnson Street, Weldon Street, and Ridge Street before finally ending at the junction of Church and Dewey.

"How could we have missed it? The road's only about half a mile," I complained.

"Perhaps it's further down that way," Bateman replied, pointing back down the road. "We might not have joined the road at the beginning."

After turning the car around and driving almost the entire

length of the same street, we had almost reached the point at which we had originally turned onto the road when I spotted something.

"How the hell did we miss that?" I shouted.

Between two eight-foot brick towers that stood amongst trees was a metal archway more than 20 feet in the air—the entrance to Magnolia Cemetery. Ironically, the cemetery was positioned a block away from the Spartanburg County Judicial Center and opposite the sheriff's office in whose car park were more than forty stationary squad cars. Never before had a lawbreaking been more open to police scrutiny than in Spartanburg.

The state of the graves in the cemetery was abysmal. Rarely had I seen vandalism on quite the same scale as in Magnolia Cemetery, and, as always, I began to speculate on the history of this bizarre law. Maybe it was simply designed to discourage pip-spitting, but since the cemetery had clearly been neglected for decades that didn't seem to make much sense. The few headstones that hadn't been toppled by vandals were still in terrible condition, bearing giant cracks and missing chunks of granite. Where walls had once existed, only partial segments of raised stone now stood. It appeared no grave had been spared the indignity. In the centre of the cemetery, however, the list of the deceased inscribed on a giant stone tablet remained perfectly intact, revealing the chilling fact that Smith was by far the most represented name in the graveyard, with thirteen graves bearing the family name.

I must admit, this was the one law I did not enjoy breaking. Originally I had planned on taking the lawbreaking to its most extreme and had envisaged a picnic in the centre of the cemetery involving watermelon sandwiches, watermelon pie, and watermelon vodka with which to wash it all down. But as I stood there, the comic appeal of the whole adventure was totally forgotten, like the memories of the people who were buried around me. I devoured the slice of watermelon quickly, reluctantly breaking the law, then started to walk back to the car. En route we passed a crypt whose door was dented and hanging off its hinges. Not a word was spoken between Bateman and me until we had returned to the car, where Bateman said what was on both of our minds.

"How can a cemetery so close to a police station be in such bad shape?"

As Bateman drove us away from Spartanburg, I attempted to rub the watermelon juice stain out of my T-shirt and totted up the score so far. Although the law was the sixteenth I had attempted to break, it was my tenth success—my crime spree had finally reached double figures. Using the laptop later on in the motel after Bateman had checked his e-mail, I discovered a further cause for celebration in the form of his reply to "Lisa." Apparently I was the best looking girl he had ever seen in his life. Lucky me.

16

DOGGY PADDLE

On the historic day when Israeli troops made their final withdrawal from the Gaza Strip thirty-eight years after capturing the narrow coastal area, and a day after the deadline for the new Iraqi constitution was extended, the front pages of the morning's national newspapers were dominated by the rather disturbing news that petrol prices in America had reached their highest-ever level, at $3 a gallon. The Americans were outraged at what they saw as highway robbery, but Bateman and I merely felt a deep sense of jealousy and amazement—it was still just half of what we paid in England.

It had been two days since the watermelon eating in Spartanburg, and now we were in Virginia, where signs warned that speeding violations were detected by aircraft. How exciting.

We were headed either to Washington, D.C., or Ocean City, Maryland, to break our next law. Based on the geography, we decided tackling Ocean City first would mean less driving overall. Plus, if we hit Washington first, we would have to travel through West Virginia in order to get there. In West Virginia, it is perfectly legal to scrape roadkill off the road and take it home for supper. Given Bateman's eagle eye for the tarmac-assisted delicacy, I feared what he might rustle up for our evening meal. That being said, we had already visited McDonald's. Compared to that ordeal, roast roadkill didn't sound too bad.

At the southern end of Virginia lies the delightfully English-sounding town of Norfolk. We had already driven through Suffolk, Portsmouth, and the counties of Isle of Wight, Southampton, and Sussex. Everything in Virginia sounded English. We passed through areas where high-rise buildings stared down at enormous yachts, the whole place exuding prosperity. It felt as if we were back amidst the rich and powerful of America once again.

It may not be the most well-known of America's landmarks, and in fact I hadn't heard of it until the name appeared on the map, but the Chesapeake Bay Bridge, which we took to reach the peninsula on which Ocean City is located, is a modern feat of engineering prowess. It may not be as long as the Seven Mile Bridge, which winds its way down the chain of Florida Keys, joining them up on its way to Key West, or as famous as the Brooklyn Bridge, which links Manhattan to its outer-borough neighbour, but what distinguishes the Chesapeake Bay Bridge—other than its confusing name which looks a lot like the word *cheapskate*—is its dramatic appearance. It is a work of distinctive and stylish elegance that would make Isambard Kingdom Brunel and other great visionaries sit up in their graves and take note.

When it was first constructed in 1964, the bridge-tunnel, which stretches 23 miles to connect southeastern Virginia to the Delmarva Peninsula, was officially named after civic leader Lucius J. Kellam, Jr. Its ingenuity lies in the fact that although the bridge stands less than 30 feet above the water, ships and boats that require a greater clearance in order to pass underneath needn't worry. After the first several miles, the bridge comes to an end on a man-made island where a tunnel, plummeting deep under the water, allows the road to continue beneath the sea for over a mile, permitting the unhampered crossing of nautical traffic far above them. The concrete island, which is one of four, is slightly larger than five acres, and from the edge of it, by the gift shop and restaurant, you can fish whilst staring at an exact replica island over a mile away, where the traffic continues over the strait and onto dry land.

With the car back on terra firma, having crossed the bridge, the peninsula was a huge contrast to the shores we had just left. Gone were the skyscrapers that lined Norfolk and Virginia Beach's coast, and the multitude of cars alongside which we had been squeezed on the bridge had suddenly and eerily disappeared, leaving us more or less alone on a quiet stretch of road where trees and the occasional house made up civilisation. We noticed a couple of shops that seemed to specialise in fireworks or peanuts, and a couple more that combined the two.

Sixty miles north, as the narrow stretch of land widened, we entered Maryland, the nineteenth state we had visited thus far. I wasn't sure what to expect from Ocean City—on the map it was just a simple dot, without the colouring used to indicate a great deal of urbanisation. Given that and the lack of nearby interstates, I imagined the town would be nothing more than a quiet, peaceful haven. I couldn't have been more wrong.

Ocean City is situated at the Maryland-Delaware border, on a narrow strip of land four streets wide and about ten miles long. Since the city's postwar boom and the addition of tons of dune sand forming a picturesque beach, it is now home to bars, restaurants, numerous hotels, and all manner of activities from mini golf and banana boat rides to horse racing and the local Ripley's Believe It or Not Museum. Far from being just a tiny Maryland backwater, as I had earlier presumed, Ocean City is one of the most popular vacation spots in the East. Unfortunately, Bateman and I were not thinking of jollity and excitement. We had hit a very uncommunicative patch in our holiday—after 33 days of constant companionship, conversations promptly ground to a halt with one-word answers or grunts. I hadn't even mentioned the dead bird I saw lying on the side of the road earlier in the afternoon, squandering a point in the game for fear of his response.

Arriving in a tourist hub in mid-August meant that, despite my coupon book, no cheap motel deals were to be found in town.

"They were asking a hundred sixty-nine dollars a night in there! I walked right out!" I said as I returned to the car to find a cheaper place to stay. "Don't know why there aren't any coupons—there are loads of hotels."

"Yeah, well, not everyone's a gypo like you!" said Bateman, who was both sleep-deprived and hungover.

"Yes, Bateman. I'm a gypsy," I remarked sarcastically.

"Things are more expensive on the coast, you know?"

"Are they?" I replied, my widened eyes upping the ante on the sarcasm.

"It *is* the summer."

"Couldn't tell by the clouds, though, could you?" I replied, trying to break the tension.

"It's still in the eighties!" Bateman snapped.

With the majority of hotels and motels asking for well over $150, we made our way back over the bridge to the mainland and a motel in West Ocean City.

Leaving Bateman to sleep off his hangover in the hope that his mood would improve, I made my way across the road from our motel and into the Ocean City Tourist Office, in which I checked mine and "Lisa's" e-mails. With there being no reply awaiting me in "Lisa's" inbox and with little else to do to keep myself entertained, I returned to the motel, grabbed my towel, and headed to the pool for a swim on my own.

After a dozen or so lengths of a peaceful and calming swim, the silence was suddenly broken by the arrival of two children who jumped in and floated on body boards they'd brought into the pool with them. Like most Americans, these boys had been raised to be polite and in no way shy—they instantly introduced themselves. Adam and Aaron weren't identical twins, but they looked the same, had similar hair-cuts, and were both equally overweight. In our brief conver-sation, I learnt that they were eight years old, both wanted to grow up to become cops, and that they had "never met a guy from where I was from" before. As I pushed myself off the wall of the pool to begin another length, Adam began to read the rules of the pool out loud.

"No running or diving; no eating or drinking around the pool; children under the age of fourteen must be . . ." The word was *accompanied,* and Adam glanced over to see if his brother was looking. He wasn't. "Um, watched by an adult."

"Accompanied," said a bold voice from over the fence. "The word is *accompanied,* son."

The man who'd made the correction entered the pool area with his wife. He turned out to be the children's grand-dad, and the two of them joined their grandchildren in the pool. Adam and Aaron introduced me to him, and we began chatting.

Vernon was from West Virginia and was very quick to dis-pel any opinion I may have formed about his family.

"I've got four grandchildren. My two little girls are straight-A students." He pointed at the twins. "And I've also got Dumb and Dumber over there."

Talking to Vernon was interesting to say the least. He seemed completely at ease, and when you're talking to a total stranger in a swimming pool wearing just a pair of shorts, you have to be. Ruth, his wife, seemed to know her place; she stood at a distance and simply agreed with every point her husband made.

"So, are you a religious man?" he asked.

"Um, no, not really. England tends to be more populated by non-church-goers nowadays," I replied.

Vernon shook his head, disappointed. "Shame, that. You've got God versus Darwin over there, haven't you?"

"Pardon?" I asked, thinking I must have missed an epic heavyweight title fight.

"People either praise God or Darwin."

"Oh, Charles Darwin—*Origin of Species* man. Well, I wouldn't say that. People believe his work, but he's not seen as a god."

"All that talk of us evolving from apes. I never used to be no monkey."

Vernon and his wife were creationists, and ever since I had learnt of the theology, I had wanted to meet a believer. Basically, creationism is the belief that humans, all other life on earth, and the universe were all created by a supernatural being. The belief is almost always coupled with a strong religious background, and Vernon certainly had that.

"But there's evidence to back Darwin up. What have you got, holy scriptures?" I asked.

Vernon and his wife scoffed at the preposterous suggestion that the Bible wasn't literal evidence of creationism. "Recently they found a bit of Noah's ark, so that proves the Bible is true, doesn't it?"

"Not really," I replied. "*If* they found it and *if* it was part of Noah's ark, then surely it means that that part of the Bible has some truth to it—but not all of it."

In addition to his adamant belief in creationism, Vernon had some strong right-wing beliefs on everything from terrorism to immigration, including the opinion that Cubans and Mexicans choose to come to America because it's the greatest nation on earth and not, as I pointed out, because it's closest.

"Abraham Lincoln once said that this country will fall from within. That's exactly what it's doing. This country has too much anger—everyone hates each other. Even my son's in jail," he remarked.

"Oh, is he?" I replied tentatively.

"Yeah. He shot his wife and her boyfriend," he said quite breezily.

"Really?" I replied in surprise. I reassured myself that shooting at someone wasn't as bad as murdering them.

"Yeah. He survived . . . she didn't." Vernon slumped and stared into the pool water. "And they sued *me*!"

"Why?" I replied, stepping back from Vernon.

"He borrowed my rifle to shoot her with. I'm telling ya, Rich, anyone can be a cop over here. You don't have to be clever."

"Is that right?" I replied. Turning to Adam and Aaron, who by now were trying to climb on the same body board, I said, "Tell me again—what do you two want to be when you grow up?"

"My name's Adam and he's Aaron," Adam replied.

Vernon shook his head and extended his arm in their direction. "See what I mean?"

By the time Bateman had arisen from his coma-like state, thankfully in a better mood, the sun had set. The lawbreaking would have to wait until the following day. That night we decided to experience the life and soul of Ocean City. When we got off the bus on the other side of the bridge, everything was reminiscent of the British seaside—minus the litter, drunkards, and donkey shit on the beach. A Ferris wheel stood forlornly abandoned, shut down for the night, just like the corkscrew roller coaster alongside. In full swing were the energetically lit amusement arcades and food carts lining the boardwalk to the beach. To complete the all-British seaside experience, the heavens opened and it began to rain. We ran to the nearest bar for shelter.

"Two beers, please," Bateman ordered. Asked for our picture IDs, we both reached into our wallets for our UK driving licences.

"Sorry, boys, it has to be a U.S. driver's licence."

"Why?" we asked. Every other place in America had accepted our licences as proof of age.

"Sorry, guys, it's bar policy."

So we couldn't drink in that bar. Big deal. There were plenty of others on the same street and we only had to run out into the rain for less than a minute to find one.

The doorman at the next place stopped us as we tried to enter. "Can I see some ID, please?" We proffered our licences once more and got a similar response: "You don't have U.S. driver's licences, do you?"

"How the hell can we have U.S. driving licences when we're English? Do you expect us to pass our U.S. driving test before we enter?" Bateman ranted as we walked away. "What's wrong with my driving licence? It's better than yours. Can you drive anywhere in the world with your driving licence? No. I bloody can!"

Our third attempt at wetting our whistle had an Irishman on the door. Surely that guaranteed victory.

"ID, please," he asked.

"OK, but I warn you, they are U.K. driving licences," I told him.

"Sorry, boys. The manager won't allow these. They have to be American."

"But you're Irish—you know these are real. What's wrong with this city? You don't live here, do you?"

"God, no," he replied.

Before we gave up and returned to the motel, we tried one final bar in the hope of a drink. Thankfully, the guy behind the bar accepted our IDs without caring what country they were from. As we discussed the difficulty we had endured in our quest for a drink, a Romanian waitress who stood by the door handing out menus and showing people to their tables leaned over to offer her expert opinion on why the Americans had not believed our ID was genuine: "Because zey are stoopid."

After a few drinks and an evening's free entertainment from a magician, we took the bus back to the motel. Bateman, however, requested that I drop him back in town with his passport. "Now we'll see who won't let me in, won't we? Bastards."

In Ocean City it is illegal to eat whilst swimming. The following day provided perfect conditions for such an activity. Clear blue skies replaced the previous night's rain, and temperatures hovered on the fringe of the 100s.

This lawbreaking escapade was likely to be the quickest one yet. At the food stand opposite Ripley's Believe It or Not Museum I purchased what can only be described as the smallest, and at $4 the most expensive, hot dog in existence and made my way towards the beach. Although I wasn't impressed by the size of the hot dog, the seagull that followed me all the way across the pier and down onto the pristine white sands of the beach certainly was—it kept ogling the food with criminal intent. Maybe it thought I was a city boy or someone from inland and would be an easy target. But it knew nothing of my background.

"You think you're going to steal my hot dog, do ya? I know your tricks; I'm from Cornwall, you know. I've been to St. Ives, where hundreds of your friends live. Don't think I don't know what you're up to," I warned.

Undeterred, the bird remained on my tail until I chased it back up the beach, wildly kicking my legs and flapping my arms in a desperate bid to show it who was boss. With the seagull out of the picture, Bateman and I were free to prepare for the lawbreaking. Bateman guarded our things while I made my way into the sea with hot dog in hand. The surf conditions weren't the greatest for swimming; choppy, three-to-four-foot waves broke haphazardly, causing the lifeguards' whistles to sound frequently as swimmers drifted perilously close to the pier's wooden structure. Strolling into the water and dropping my shoulder to combat the breaking waves, I placed the hot dog in my mouth and began with a touch of breaststroke, receiving a strange look from the lady I greeted as I passed.

"Good mormin," I mumbled.

"Um, hi," she replied before swimming quickly to her friend and pointing in my direction.

Due to the hot dog's minimal size, I finished it in two bites and body-surfed a wave back into shore.

"That'll do me, Bateman," I remarked, drying myself off. "Let's get out of this town that refuses to sell us alcohol."

As I searched through my pockets for the keys to the car, the woman and her family, who were sitting behind us and had seen my arrival, quick swim, and preparations for departure, stared blankly at me.

Soon we were on our way north and into Delaware, where the world of hoteliers and restaurateurs returned back to state parks and the feel of England once more. Counties of Sussex and Middlesex greeted us in Delaware and so did the road to Washington, D.C. Up until now I'd been breaking laws that seemed stupid and old-fashioned because they had been drafted to serve a purpose that became obsolete countless years ago. But in our next destination, America's capital city, I intended to break a law that wasn't passed until the turn of the twenty-first century.

17

LET'S GO
FLY A KITE

Before leaving England amidst the anticipation and excitement generated by the press coverage, I had been warned about only one of the 25 laws I had intended to break. Ever since the September 11 atrocities, the U.S. authorities have been vehemently strict about what does and does not enter American airspace. Without prior permission, nothing is allowed to fly over the nation's capital—not even, as it turns out, a kite. That was the law I planned to violate.

Bateman and I were only too happy to leave our downtown motel early in the morning. The previous evening Bateman had left the motel in search of a shop in which to buy some cigarettes, and upon his return to the room he quickly bolted every lock. It turned out he'd run into some dangerous-looking types on the street who'd said some threatening things to him.

"I didn't think I was ever gonna get out of that alive. This is a dangerous place, mate."

With Washington mornings seeming far less menacing, Bateman and I checked out of the motel, the task ahead uppermost in our minds. We stepped out of the building into a day of tremendous heat without a breath of wind—not ideal kite-flying conditions.

Driving through the open streets of Washington and passing the White House several times in an attempt to find somewhere to park, what I first noticed about the city was that there were more presidential memorials and museums dedicated to celebrated Americans than you could shake a stick at. At every pedestrian crossing, we waited patiently as hordes of tourists swept past us on a well-worn (and signposted) trail to the next monument. We parked on Fourth Street in a spot not far from the National Mall—an avenue of grass where the phallic-shaped Washington Monument stood at one end with the United States Capitol over a mile away at the other. Two of America's most iconic buildings were now equidistant from our car, with just a turn of the head needed to capture the two. More importantly, on the Mall I had more than enough room in which to run with a kite. All I needed now was to find one.

The trouble with Washington is that when the countless monuments were being built, it appears they used so much material that none was left to build shops and other city amenities. On the walk to the Washington Monument from the car I can only remember passing the national art, American history, and natural history museums, and as we walked from there to the White House the only thing that resembled a shop was a bank and a number of souvenir stands that sold tacky "I ♥ Washington" T-shirts—and at that moment in time, I certainly didn't ♥ the place.

After threading our way through the mass of people who stood outside the gates of the White House, all waiting futilely for a chance to photograph their friends and family without some passerby entering the shot, Bateman and I retraced our steps in search of a lamppost banner I had seen that advertised the city's shopping district: the Golden Triangle, which was supposed to have six hotels, twenty restaurants, and six hundred shops. Surely there was a kite hiding somewhere in there.

After an hour in the Golden Triangle, all we'd found of interest was a Subway, which provided us with sandwiches for lunch. We emerged from the restaurant into the extreme heat, which caused my feet to sweat so much that my flip-flops were beginning to squeak with every step I took. I visited an electronics store next door in the hope that one of the employees could assist me in my hunt for a kite.

"Excuse me. You wouldn't know of anywhere I could buy a kite, would you?"

"A kite?" replied the woman, almost choking on her chewing gum. I might as well have asked if I could buy a Soviet nuclear warhead. "No, I don't know any kite shops."

"Well, I'm not looking for a kite shop. I'm sure I won't find one of them, just a place that might sell a kite."

"No, sorry, sir. There's a guy on the corner whose job it is to help shoppers find their way around the Triangle, though. He would know."

The man in question stood at the end of the street and, befitting the name of the area in which he worked, was dressed in gold.

"Yes, sir. May I help you?"

"Yes, I'm wondering if you know of any place that might sell a kite."

"A kite?"

What was it with a kite? I know it's not the most commonly requested item but it wasn't as bizarre as the responses I'd gotten would suggest. Maybe buying kites was as illegal as flying them.

The man consulted his clipboard.

"I'll have to radio HQ," he replied, and raised his walkie-talkie to his mouth. "We have a gentleman requesting a kite."

The radio crackled before a voice responded: "A kite?"

By that point I was thinking that it might be less of a

bother to find a shop that sold stuffed penguins wearing Bermuda shorts and a removable welder's mask. Just then a lady who had obviously overheard my request approached me and, as always, asked Bateman and me to say a few words in our British accents—those American girls do seem to love the sound of it. I obliged, then I asked her to return the favour.

"You don't know anywhere I can buy a kite, do you?"

"No."

A similar response came from the guide when HQ finally got back in contact with him. The Golden Triangle: six hotels, twenty restaurants, six hundred shops, zero kites.

"Let's go back to the car and find a Wal-Mart, mate. They've always helped us out in the past. They'll have a kite, they're bound to," I said confidently. Bateman didn't look too convinced.

We drove over the Potomac River and into Virginia, sticking to Route 1, which we were sure would take us to some sort of shopping complex. In Target, a store that is similar to Wal-Mart in nearly every way other than the uniform of the employees, Vladimir was the first person who didn't question my intentions and led me to where he was sure he had seen such an item before.

"It was right here," he said, pointing at a shelf now dominated by Barbie products.

"Hey, I don't even mind if it's a Barbie kite, mate," I replied in desperation.

Valdimir wandered off to speak to a colleague. When he returned, he was shaking his head. "No, there are no kites here. Sorry."

"Can you tell me where the nearest Wal-Mart is, please?"

"Yes, yes. Just stick to Route One."

Several miles down, with no Wal-Mart in sight, we passed another Target but thought it wiser to continue on in hopes of finding a Wal-Mart, as it had never let us down in the past. At the next shopping complex I asked a man pushing a trolley if he knew where the superstore was. Unfortunately, he couldn't speak English, and so I moved on to a boy in his teens, who did his best to inform me that "it may be down there." Strange that in the nation's capital, hardly anyone spoke English. As it turned out, Wal-Mart *was* "down there" and was actually the next building along, a hundred yards away.

Entering the store, I ran instantly to the toy department and was greeted by a woman who, luckily, spoke perfect English.

"Excuse me, but I was wondering if you sold kites. I've been looking for one for hours."

"We do." The news almost dropped me to my knees. My search was almost at an end.

"Just not at this time of year," she continued. Shit.

"Right, that's it!" I shouted at Bateman before storming down one of the many aisles.

"You giving up?" he asked. I must admit, I had thought about it, but if I succeeded in breaking this law it would be four on the trot, something I hadn't yet achieved.

"No. I'm going to make one."

"What?"

"Come on, it can't be that difficult. I made one at school once. It didn't fly, but I'm older and wiser now—I'm sure I can do better this time. What stuff do I need? It's all here."

Although it didn't look like it when the items where scanned by Sue at the checkout, the very economical $3.74 worth of items my basket contained were all I needed to construct the perfect kite.

Now, children, this is what you'll need to make your very own kite in a shopping centre car park just outside Washington, D.C.:

- A packet of ten bin liners
- A carton of seventy-five drinking straws
- Some sticky tape
- The remaining catgut you used to try to catch a fish with a lasso in Tennessee
- A pair of scissors (but do ask an adult to do any of the cutting)

1. Return to car and place bin bag on boot of vehicle. The wind that has by now picked up will create bad kite preparation conditions but will no doubt aid the eventual flight attempt once you return to the city.

2. To the best of your ability, cut a square shape out of the bin liner (it's best if you cut along the seams of the liner, which will then open out into such a shape).

3. As your assistant holds the frame of the kite, count how many straws will be needed to line the frame of the kite in an X across its reverse.

4. By squeezing the end of the straws, you can insert them into each other to make one big straw, which will hopefully reach from one top corner to its opposite bottom corner. Repeat procedure for the two remaining corners.

5. Once the straw frames have been made, fasten them down with sticky tape. This will now act as the kite's support and will stop it from simply folding under pressure from the wind.

6. Tell any passersby who may have heard you talk in your English accent and want you say a few words that "the only thing that springs to mind is: I'd love to but can't you see I'm busy making a kite?"

7. Cut four equal lengths of catgut (a good measurement is the distance between Bateman's foot and the bridge of his nose).

8. Fasten the ends of the four lengths of catgut to each of

the corners of the bin liner with sticky tape and collect the four other ends in your right or left hand.

9. Return to Washington, feeling ever so slightly proud of your accomplishment.

Upon our return to the city through the rush-hour traffic (we seemed to be plagued by it no matter how hard we tried to avoid it), we parked just opposite the Mall, and I made my way onto the freshly cut grass with kite in hand. The wind, which had not helped during the making of the kite, had suddenly disappeared when it came to the only time of day when its presence was an absolute necessity. Even the dozens of American flags surrounding the Washington Monument over half a mile away were drooping or motionless. What was worse was the discovery that somewhere during the transportation of the kite from Wal-Mart to the Mall, it had somehow lost a piece of catgut, leaving my kite with only three lines.

"Run with it!" Bateman shouted, camera in hand, ready to capture the moment.

Taking Bateman's advice, I ran towards the monument until the heat and my lack of fitness tired me out. I needn't have even tried—the kite simply dragged along the ground, rising no higher than a couple of feet—which caused some of the straw framework to begin to come loose.

10. Ensure that your kite isn't a badly made piece of crap.

Undeterred, I returned to the car to make adjustments to the straws, then made my way back onto the grass for a final attempt. As I walked down to the centre of the Mall, I felt a breeze on my neck and instantly sprang into action. I unfolded the kite, clutched the three remaining strings, and threw the liner up into the air, where it was picked up by a gust of wind. With the kite at full extension of the strings and with my arms at full stretch, the kite must have soared to at least 15 feet and looked as majestic in its upwards surge as an eagle in full flight—well, as much as a bin liner with sixteen coloured straws attached can resemble a bird of prey. Although Bateman didn't manage to capture the brief moment of flight on film, at least the law was broken and I'd achieved four successes in a row. Four on the trot was like a dream come true. In the searing heat, amidst complete strangers staring at the sight of me and my bin liner, I felt ever so slightly heroic and stood as proudly as the monument at the end of the Mall.

"To the car, Bateman. Our work here is complete."

Despite the rush-hour traffic and plenty of wrong turns, we managed to find Interstate 270, which would carry us north towards our next destination. We pulled off and stayed in a motel in a small town called Hagerstown, which lies just south of Maryland's border with Pennsylvania. It was time to check how well Bateman and "Lisa's" long-distance relationship was blossoming. From what Bateman had written it was coming on in leaps and bounds—so well, in fact, that Bateman had asked what "Lisa" was doing the week after I was due to fly home. As luck would have it, it was "Lisa's" week off then, and if Bateman wanted to, he was free to spend a week in sunny Indianapolis with her and frequent the local nightspots.

Bateman's e-mail wasn't the only fresh message in my inbox that evening. Surprisingly, the second was more of a joy to read. It was from a gentleman by the name of Kevin Harvey, who represented the picture desk of the *Metro* newspaper in London. He explained that he was very interested in my "unique crime spree" and my "proposed underwater bike ride along the river Thames." What on earth was he talking about? I replied to Kevin, questioning the origin of the biking rumour, then sat back and told Bateman about the bizarre message I had just received. He didn't seem too bothered. Mind you, he had just found out he could stay in Indianapolis for free.

For the first time on the holiday, I wasn't thinking about what law I was planning on breaking the following day. Instead, I focused on what I might do when I returned home. Riding a bike underwater along the river Thames? What a bloody good idea.

18
SUITE DREAMS

In the brochure rack at our motel in Hagerstown were adverts for a nearby outlet mall: Prime Outlets of Hagerstown. Having never been to an outlet mall before, I thought it would be at the very least an ideal chance to buy some cheap clothes and presents for friends and family back home, so we decided to leave travelling to Pittsburgh for later on in the morning and concentrate on visiting the mall first and foremost.

With Hagerstown being just a minor outpost on Maryland's border with Pennsylvania, I was surprised when we had to wait for over five minutes just to join the queue of traffic that had developed near our motel. When the congestion eased and we began to make our way under the interstate and towards the outlet mall, there were no clues as to why traffic had come to a standstill for such a prolonged amount of time. As we edged closer to the top of a hill before taking the appropriate turnoff, we saw a petrol station with an unusual number of motorcycles filling up—four in all, and another five waiting to visit the pumps. A moment later, we heard a deafening roar, and saw through a break in the traffic dozens of motorcycles heading towards the mall.

Our eventual arrival into the mall's car park was one of the most surreal experiences of my life. The motorcycles we had first seen in the petrol station and crossing the road were just a handful of the hundreds and hundreds of motorcycles parked there, and still more filtered through from all directions. Harley-Davidsons, Yamahas, Suzukis, and Hondas all appeared, along with the biggest collections of moustaches and bandanas ever seen in one place. Thinking it was either some sort of world-record attempt or a Hell's Angels reunion, Bateman and I stood in reverence, the overall roar of the engines growing in power and volume as more and more bikes joined the procession. The bikers who had arrived already gave one another pats on the back and enjoyed some food or drink at the trailers that had been set up for that purpose.

As we locked the car and made our way towards the horde of bikers in an attempt to find out why they had convened in such great numbers in such an insignificant town, we passed what Bateman described as "the coolest bike of the lot." Away from any other bikes, so it could be admired by all, was a Harley-style bike with perfectly burnished engine and valves gleaming beneath the American flag emblazoned on its side.

(Days later, in a motel room several states away, I picked up the room's television remote control and witnessed a live news report from New York on Fox News. It appeared that the bikers' Fifth Annual 9/11 Commemorative Ride had come to a successful finale in the Big Apple—and the featured bike, next to which the reporter stood, was the Stars and Stripes bike I had seen in Hagerstown.)

The outlet mall was basically laid out like a little town, with the exception that the grouping of shops had only pedestrian thoroughfares and was surrounded by an enormous car park, which by now was at bursting point due to the motorbike manifestation.

In the Adidas outlet store I purchased a pair of trousers and a shirt (a bargain at $30) and began talking to the sales assistant about the most pressing matter on my mind.

"Why are there about a thousand motorbikes parked in the car park?"

She peered through the automatic doors as if to check I wasn't just making it up. "I'm not really sure. I haven't heard anything about it," she replied. "I love your accent. What are you doing over here?"

Throughout the trip, I found that the most difficult question to answer. If I was in a pub or a place where I was settled and in the mood for a string of questions related to the origin and highlights of my journey, I would always give a truthful response. In small-talk situations, I tried to be vaguer. It never worked in small towns, though—the residents always seemed shocked that a tourist might choose to visit their town.

"Oh, I'm just travelling around America," I replied coyly.

"Why the hell did you come *here*?" No difference here then.

Queuing at one of the food courts, where nearly every fast-food chain is represented, I happened to catch a glimpse of the back of a man's T-shirt, which seemed to suggest the reason for the motorcyclists' grand gathering. As his ponytail waved from side to side, revealing more of the text, it appeared that Hagerstown was a major stop-off on the Fifth Annual 9/11 Commemorative Rides, this year's course had taken them from North Carolina to Philadelphia and would finish in New York City in a couple of days' time. As I sat down and joined Bateman at one of the food court's tables, describing what I had read and taking one final glance at the man's shirt, a thought suddenly dawned on me. Although it was August, which straightaway seemed the incorrect month to commemorate something that had happened in September, it struck me as even odder that the Fifth Annual 9/11 Commemorative Ride was taking place in 2005, less than four years since the Twin Towers disaster.

An hour after arriving, our shopping done and our stomachs filled, we were set to leave and make our way to Pittsburgh—but it seemed the bikers had picked the same time for their departure to Philadelphia. Fifteen minutes of revving engines and gusts of exhaust fumes later, all but a few of the bikers had vanished (along with the news helicopter that had been circling to monitor their every move), leaving the car park forlorn and godforsaken. It was time to embark north and into Pennsylvania, where the day was only going to become stranger, as I hoped to wake up the following morning on top of a fridge.

Without any overwhelming need to rush, and with me being a cheapskate, we decided to stay off the toll interstate roads common in the built-up areas of the East. We passed through towns named Accident, Laboratory, and my personal favourite, Eighty Four. *Strange American Town Names* and *America's Greatest Roundabouts*—two fascinating TV series that are just waiting for the BBC to snap them up.

It's always nice to enter a new state, especially one I've never visited before. By this stage, we had a comfortable routine: cross the border, visit the rest area and connecting tourist information centres that always instantly follows a border crossing, and instantly find a new motel coupon book. Pennsylvania's rest area was set back from the road, surrounded by trees and boasting a statue of one of the state's first governors. The coupon book could help me find a hotel within the city limits of Pittsburgh that could guarantee to have a refrigerator.

Home to America's original capital city, Philadelphia, the Keystone State is also home to two of the most amusing laws I had come across. In Pennsylvania, a law clearly drafted at the time of the introduction of the automobile states that if a motorist sees a horse approaching, the person must cover the car in a blanket or canvas that blends into its surroundings, and then allow the horse to pass. If the horse still appears skittish, the motorist must take the car apart piece by piece and hide it under the nearest tree. That law was too easy to break, of course. I'd simply have to leave my car intact in the presence of a horse, something I was sure every Pennsylvanian does anyway. However, I was pretty sure that very few people had ever slept on top of a refrigerator, and for that reason alone I was heading for Pittsburgh.

Only four miles from the centre of the city, our motel seemed to be light-years away from any sort of civilisation. With not even a single branch of any fast-food chain on the horizon, and only a petrol station and equally bleak accommodations nearby, we randomly chose a motel at the top of a barren hill whose most distinguishing attribute was a plentiful supply of roadkill lying on the road at the bottom of the hill. Normally a motel coupon's discount price would be honored only on weekdays, but by the empty look of the car park outside the Comfort Inn, we were hoping that at this, one of the few motels with a refrigerator, our weekend stay would be discounted as well.

Danielle, the motel's receptionist, was watching the Golf Channel as I entered with coupon book in hand.

"Sorry to interrupt you but I was wondering how much a double room for this evening would be," I said. "I've got a coupon."

"Sorry," came her reply. "It really only counts for Sunday through Thursdays. A room will be eighty dollars."

"Eighty dollars?" I asked, brandishing the coupon, which discounted the rate to $60 on other days of the week. "Can't you do me some sort of Englishman deal?" I added as Bateman joined me in the foyer.

Danielle smiled and looked at the screen of her computer. "Seeing as I like your accents, how about a room for eighty dollars and I'll give you a room with a Jacuzzi, normally priced at a hundred twenty?"

"Sure," I replied. "Has it got a fridge?"

"A refrigerator you mean?"

"Well, it's just easier to say fridge. That's what we call it back home."

"All of our rooms have . . . um . . . fridges."

"Follow me. I'll show you to your room," Danielle said. We trailed after her eagerly. Up to now we'd stayed in our fair share of dismal hovels, but our own Jacuzzi room was going to make up for the lot of them (even if I was to spend the night in the most uncomfortable of places).

"Here it is. King-size bed, desk, Jacuzzi, and . . ." She looked puzzled. "There doesn't seem to be a pull-out bed, just an armchair and footrest." I didn't mind—the room had a decent-sized fridge, and that was all I cared about.

"That doesn't matter. I'll take it," I replied.

"I can find a room with a pull-out if you want, but it won't have a Jacuzzi."

"I don't mind sleeping in the armchair," Bateman voiced.

"You'll be on the bed, won't you," I remarked, tilting my head towards the fridge and raising my eyebrows to remind Bateman of just why we were here, but maybe giving Danielle a completely different image in her mind.

"Oh. OK, then," Danielle remarked, almost running out the door.

The armchair, footrest, and fridge (once it had been disconnected from the wall, dragged across the floor, and laid on its side) were almost the same height and, pieced together, formed my "bed" for the night. Once a blanket had been placed on top, it didn't look or feel too uncomfortable, and I was positive I had slept in more awkward positions after a night of heavy drinking than on top of a fridge—in a phone box and under a car being two that sprang instantly to mind.

"You're gonna like this, Bateman. The only way I'm going to be able to sleep on this fridge tonight is by getting hammered, so I won't care where I sleep. Pub?"

I didn't have to ask him twice.

Unfortunately for us, the pub was at the very bottom of the very steep hill on which the motel was situated, and walking right on the main road seemed the only way of getting to it. Walking anywhere else was virtually impossible, as it meant wading through long shoots of grass that probably had an assortment of venomous creatures, so we carefully made our way along the road, cars hurtling along just inches from us. If it was this terrifying when I was sober, I thought, there was no guarantee I would even make it back to the motel when I'd drunk enough alcohol to make the prospect of sleeping on a fridge appealing.

In the pub, as we dove into our first pint, I quickly pulled out the book and made doubly sure that the law stated it was illegal to sleep *on* a refrigerator, not *in* one.

As was the case with so many evenings in America, I found it difficult to remember the finer points of what occurred that evening. Bateman and I definitely had some sort of deep and profound conversation about something, but I can't recall whether it was about forming our own country or what it would be like to be reincarnated as a limpet.

I can say that three things definitely happened. Bateman

and I both enjoyed chicken Caesar salads, which were advertised as "salads as big as your head." Secondly, I must have been extremely drunk, as I have no memory whatsoever of my presumably treacherous walk back up to our motel. The third thing is the way Bateman woke me in the middle of the night.

"Bateman?" I said, lifting my face off of my drool-drenched pillow. "Why are you in the Jacuzzi with all of your clothes on? You're bloody soaking."

"I dunno. I must have fallen in," he sniggered.

"Is that the camera you have in your hand? It bloody is—don't drop it in the water. Why the hell have you got it, anyway?"

"I was taking a picture of you. I've taken two, actually. You should be happy I remembered. I had to go to the car to get the camera."

"But why?"

"I thought you'd want a picture of you passed out on a fridge."

I'd passed out on the fridge? Excellent.

19
FORE-
BIDDEN

August 21 was the only day on the holiday I wasn't looking forward to, and when the day finally arrived I felt a wave of homesickness. It was inevitable, and I'd expected it since I had first realised I would be in America on that particular Sunday. It wasn't that I missed my family or friends; rather, August 21 is when the residents of my home village celebrate Portreath Harbour Fun Day. Although it is primarily aimed at children and tourists—local fishermen offer free boat trips around the bay, the "greasy pole" is positioned high above the centre of the harbour and climbed by children who swing pillows wildly at each other in an attempt to knock their opponents into the water below, and the entrants of the raft race have to endure being used for target practice by spectators throwing eggs and flour from above— the local ideology is that the day should be treated as an all-day drinking marathon. All in all, Harbour Fun Day is loved and despised in equal measure by the locals, and I was saddened to be so far from an event I haven't missed since I drank three bottles of red wine in forty-five minutes in 1998 and passed out at two in the afternoon, not waking up until the following morning.

To compensate for our absence on the special day, it was

decided that we should be near water, and even if we weren't going to drink, the very least we could do was to enjoy ourselves, take a day off, and do something different. It's for this reason that I was awake early in my motel less than five miles from Niagara Falls, New York, where our very own unique Harbour Fun Day would be spent.

There are two towns called Niagara Falls, both named after the waterfall. Niagara Falls, New York, is a rather unimpressive town of cheap tourist attractions and casinos. It sits opposite the Niagara River from the Canadian town of Niagara Falls, Ontario, which far outdid the Americans' half-assed attempt to lure tourists. On the Canadian side, million-dollar hotels and observation towers stood amongst pristine gardens and neatly pruned hedges.

We parked outside a church flying the English flag on top of its tower and made our way towards the falls. En route we continued our new game—our own quiz on events in America.

"OK, then," I began. "In what town did you go missing when you ended up with that tart?"

"I can't remember, I was pissed."

"It was Grand Island. What country did Joye's mother come from?"

"I dunno."

"Honduras. You're not very good at this, are you, Bateman?"

Bateman glared at me.

"OK, then," I went on. "What was the name of the bird who met us at the Indianapolis radio station?" I took a few steps back so Bateman couldn't see the smile that was growing on my face. "Um . . . it wasn't Lisa, was it?"

"Yeah," Bateman droned.

"How did you remember that?" I asked.

Bateman turned to me, prepared for the biggest gloat of his life.

"I've been e-mailing her since we left, and I might go over there and see her when you fly home and before I go to Miami."

"Really? Well, I wouldn't bother if I were you, mate."

"Why not? She seems really up for it."

"Yeah, but 'Lisa' of indianaradiogirl@hotmail.com is me, mate."

Bateman paused for a second or two before pronouncing his opinion on the matter.

"Prick."

"Hey, you should be thankful. I could have made you fly all the way to Indianapolis, you know."

"Yeah, and if you did, I would have beaten the piss out of you."

Niagara Falls is actually three waterfalls, of which American Falls and Horseshoe Falls are the better known (Bridal Veil Falls completes the group). From where we had parked, a labyrinth of bridges and river crossings led over the river's tributaries. Seeing the gentle flow of the river and the peaceful woodland surroundings, you would never believe that you stood just seconds away from a 188-foot cascade so powerful and dramatic that a permanent cloud of spray rises higher than the top of the falls.

Horseshoe Falls is by far the most impressive of the three, probably because 90 percent of the Niagara River's water is driven over its precipice. Below, tour boats take tourists of every creed and colour as close as they possibly can to the foot of the falls, positioned on the very brink of certain destruction and where the conditions must be similar to a wind and rain-swept gale of epic proportions. From there, they can witness the magnificent sight of 600,000 gallons of water plunging every second from the 2,200-foot-long rim of the falls like an azure tablecloth draped over jagged rocks.

Bateman and I made our way over the Rainbow Bridge and into Canada, where the best views of the Horseshoe Falls are. Still more than half a mile away and 200 feet above the base, I began to feel the spray from the falling water and stopped walking, returning to the bridge back to the United States where there was no danger of clothes saturation.

Coming back across the bridge, we joined the back of the queue for U.S. immigration. Entering Canada was simple—proffer your passport and answer the usual questions, the whole process taking no longer than a minute. Returning to the States is an entirely different experience. For starters, it costs 50 cents. As we waited in line, not a single queuing person was being seen by officials, and we could hear an immigration officer shouting at someone about a pram. A family sitting by us looked terribly anxious, and I wondered if they were the cause of the temporary halt. When we were finally seen, we were eyed with suspicion and distrust and greeted in the usual obnoxious and unwelcoming way.

"And when did you last travel in the United States, sir?"

"About fifteen minutes ago. I only popped over to see the falls."

"What have you brought with you?"

"Just my wallet and passport. I had a hot dog but I've eaten that."

With no further line of questioning available to him, he allowed me to reenter the United States, calling the next person in line forward to brighten his day. Stepping out of the office and back onto American soil, I quickly calculated that we'd spent more time in the immigration office than we had at the falls. Bateman reckoned that as he had now been to

Canada, this marked the beginning of his second trip to America.

With Harbour Fun Day over for another year, it was time to concentrate again on the lawbreaking. Approximately 300 miles southeast of Niagara lay Albany, the capital of New York State, where it is illegal to play golf in the streets of the city.

I've been known to play a round or two of golf in my time, and my dad plays it religiously. To be honest, I'm not very good, and I don't see the point in traipsing round a large field looking for a ball in wintry conditions. It's still a surprise to me how the game caught on in the first place and why people took seriously a Scotsman who thought trying to get a small ball into a slightly larger hole 400 yards away was a good idea. To make it even more difficult, he placed patches of sand and water in the way. They must have thought he was mental.

Not wanting to spend more than ten or so dollars on a golf set, I opted for the rather less sporting option of visiting Toys "R" Us and purchasing the cleverly named Beginners Golf Set. Luckily for me, the quality kit not only included a club and several balls but even came complete with its own holes (little rings) and flags at which to aim.

Albany's state capitol was unlike any of the others we had seen. In Salt Lake City, Indianapolis, and other U.S. cities, you basically find a scaled-down model of the United States capitol in Washington—Greek-style stone pillars with a domed roof. Albany's is as exuberant as the Casino de Monte Carlo and is similar in appearance to a Bavarian castle, surrounded by corporate buildings and museums in what appeared to be a very affluent area of the city. Lining State Street, where all of the buildings were placed, was the largest collection of food vending vans I have ever seen in my life—and I've been to more than my fair share of car boot sales and fairgrounds. They all had something different to offer. The standard breakfast roll and hot dog vans competed with Greek, Italian, and Turkish foods, plus some other cuisines I couldn't pronounce, never mind identify. They all tried to lure the many workers who had flocked out of nearby office buildings to spend their lunch breaks in the park. This seemed the ideal location to begin the making of a country club's golf course—albeit only one hole.

The following description of the hole is best read in the style of Peter Alliss commentating at the beginning of the British Open. Listen as he talks you through this tricky 90-yarder. The raised edge of the sidewalk and the steps of the Albany Board of Education building provide the ideal location for the tee-off of this tricky par six at the Downtown Albany Country Club. From here, the golfer attempts to avoid traffic and pedestrians and can feel proud of himself if his ball lands on the opposite sidewalk instead of hooking into the construction yard to the left of the fairway. Similarly, a slice to the right risks hitting the curry and kebab vans, which are targets worth evading. Across the road, at the foot of the capitol, the hole follows the path of a nasty dogleg, where the ball should be kept to the right at all times, avoiding the building's fountain, which supplies the most picturesque of water hazards. From here, the choice to go for the green is an awfully tempting one but very often players have fallen short, leaving them with the difficult shot of having to loft the ball over the park bench and onto the green above. Two simple putts, made more taxing by the absence of a putter in the set, and that should conclude the hole and the round, with the law having been broken. Time to tee off.

Bateman made a grand caddy even if he didn't have any clubs to carry. My first shot (with a slight hook) was rather impressive—the ball drifted past the construction site and, amazingly, to the feet of the capitol's steps. On my next shot I had to avoid the fountain, however, or Bateman would force me to evoke the play-it-where-it-lies rule for a cheap laugh.

As I swung the club back, I was distracted by people both behind and in front of where I stood.

"Hang on," Bateman voiced. "People coming down the steps."

Some dignitaries walking down the steps from the capitol examined me curiously as they made their way across the road and away from the vans—they were people important enough to turn their nose up at a pork sandwich. After that, we were further delayed while two security guards crossed the "fairway," staring vacantly at me but not batting a single eyelid between them.

My swing hoisted the ball high into the air, but it dropped short and to the right of the fountain. Shot number three would need to be struck with precision and some power if it was to clear the bench and have enough flight to force its way onto the plateau where the hole was positioned. Unluckily, my strike left the ball short of the green and directly in front of the bench, which by this time was in use by a man who had sat down to eat his lunch. If my sand wedge couldn't clear his sandwich as well as him, I was in trouble—not only from the man himself for interrupting his lunch, but because it would almost certainly send me over par. Throwing caution to the wind, I hit the bottom of the ball firmly, and the ball cleared the bench, gentleman, and green quite convincingly. A quick and safe approach shot to the green left me with a single putt for par—a shot that would have been successfully taken care of if a putter was up for selection. Without it, I hopelessly chipped the ball over the hole before tapping it for seven. One over par.

The day's result wasn't too disheartening. So what if I had ended the round with a seven and not the required six? All I needed to know was that the breaking of law twenty had been a success and left me with fourteen victories overall, with six in a row. Picking my ball out of the hole and waving to the crowd, which apparently couldn't care less about what I was doing, I packed the kit back into the car and decided what to do next. The nineteenth hole (or in my case the second) was the preferred option for celebration, and without needing a great deal of persuading from Bateman, we settled for post-round potations at Hooters.

With the round being celebrated in the best way possible, in the beautiful surroundings that only Hooters girls can provide, and with my two-week-old goatee now looking pretty impressive, Bateman and I toasted the next and final stage of our journey. The following day we would set off north, through Vermont and New Hampshire. Our plan was to travel on the interstate until we reached New Hampshire's capital, Concord, where the population stood at a comparatively sparse forty thousand and the state capitol was a dull carbon copy of Washington's. From there we would take smaller roads down to Boston.

The prospect of seeing New England was exciting enough, but I was looking forward to the next law for one simple reason. It would end with the removal of my goatee, which I was just itching to shave off.

20

THE BOSTON GOATEE PARTY

On every previous visit I'd made to the States, for one reason or another, I had missed New England completely. It's one of the only places in the country I had always wanted to visit and yet had never made a conscious effort to do so. The book of stupid laws had only three good ones in New England, but I was glad that fate had finally delivered me to an area of the country I hadn't seen before.

Just as I'd imagined, New England was beautiful—witness New Hampshire's expanses of woodland, which surrounded every road we travelled on, flowing like an undulating wave of luscious green until meeting the blue sky of the horizon. The towns through which the road weaved felt home-like and familiar, and I was sure I had seen them before in American family movies at Christmastime—places where everyone knows everyone else and where the local postmaster is also the town mayor. It was in a town like this, where we pulled over to refuel, that I realised just how visually stunning this part of eastern America is. Below me was a river that passed gently under a bridge connecting the eastern and western parts of the town; above me stood a mass of trees that appeared as if it could easily swallow every building in the town. After paying for the fuel, I noticed that the station sold salt-and-vinegar-flavoured crisps, which I had failed to find in any other state until now.

Instead of taking the interstate directly to Boston, we decided to make our way to the coast and then down the Atlantic seaboard before entering Massachusetts. Just south of Portsmouth and less than twenty miles from the border with Massachusetts, stood the town of Rye Beach, a little village just north of the larger settlement of Hampton. Bateman and I decided to spend a bit of time here, as it was the first time I had seen the sea since leaving Los Angeles and the first time I'd seen the Atlantic since I had left home.

Rye Beach was how time at the seaside ought to be spent. Children dug holes on the beach, using the upturned piles of sand as makeshift forts and castles; there were no pier and no amusement arcades, it was a half-mile walk to the nearest refreshment providers, and the only sources of entertainment were the sea and sand themselves.

After a surprisingly cold swim, I returned to our spot on the beach, where I could hear an ice cream van play "The Entertainer" over and over again until all the children had purchased their frozen desserts and the van departed, only to appear at the next road that greets the beach and repeat the routine. Then the van appeared no more than 20 yards from me. I awaited the dulcet tones of "Greensleeves" or a stirring rendition of "When the Saints Come Marching In" to resonate around the beach. Even "The Birdie Song" would have been an improvement on a tune I'd heard dozens of times already.

"If I hear that tune one more pissing time, Bateman, there's gonna be big trouble in little Rye Beach."

"When are we gonna go, anyway? I get bored just lying on the beach," he replied. Just then the van reappeared a few dozen yards further down the beach.

"Now. Quickly!"

• • •

Technically, as soon as I entered Massachusetts sporting my goatee, I had broken the law, but I felt that simply crossing the border wasn't good enough. I wanted to have my picture taken somewhere memorable, somewhere that oozed Massachusetts. Like with the beer out of a bucket in St. Louis, which I did with the foreboding presence of the Gateway Arch behind me, the goatee picture had to be taken somewhere special.

Ruling out Cape Cod as "too far away" (me) and "too boring" (Bateman), we decided we would find a decent motel on the outskirts of Boston and explore the city the following day, treating the goatee to a nice day out. The motel we eventually found at least met one of my two criteria—it was on the outskirts.

After a few days without a drop of alcohol I knew it was only a matter of time until Bateman demanded we go drinking, and as he rose from his bed and reached for his shoes, I was pretty sure what he was about to suggest.

We settled for a pub just down the road from our motel that had free snacks at the bar and was showing the Boston Red Sox game on the big-screen TV. On previous trips, I stayed clear of any establishment with a baseball game, but after several weeks in the country I had developed a liking for their version of English rounders; what's more, Boston's team were the current champions of the World Series.

After several pints and being joined at the bar by a tramp who had used his collection of coins to buy a drink, play keno, lose, finish his drink, and go again, Bateman and I were refused service on the grounds that we had had too much to drink already. I would have understood if there was evidence to back up the bartender's claim, but we were sitting quietly in our chairs, weren't abusive in any way, could hold a civilised conversation (which in this case was "Why can't we have another drink?"), and came from a country where if you had managed to drag yourself to the bar under your own steam and you pronounced what beverage you required reasonably well, that was testament enough that you could still manage another drink or two.

"OK," said Bateman to the lady behind the bar. "We'll just go to another bar, then." So we did. To the one next door.

Unlike the previous bar, our new Boston local was dimly lit, the baseball was shown on a tiny screen in the corner, and everyone inside seemed depressed about something or another. I loved it—this was like a British pub. Bateman, obviously still annoyed by our experience in the first bar, took it upon himself to upgrade our level of drinking and ordered a couple of whiskies. After a few rounds of those, I would have had no quarrel with the barman asking us to leave, and I turned my attention to a games machine in the corner of the bar, which involved hitting a penguin with a baseball bat.

Like most pubs, once I had reached level two, a gentleman appeared over my shoulder to offer his opinion on how the game should be played.

"You should play the poker game, buddy," he said.

"Nah, I'm quite happy hitting this penguin into the middle of next week, thanks."

He was one of those guys who no one likes: the kind who appears over your shoulder and offers you advice on gambling machines or who comes up to the pool table and instructs you about how to hit the cue ball to gain perfect position for your next shot. The man turned out to be called Eric, whom Bateman had met earlier and who was now offering us a lift to a nearby club.

"Come on, Rich. He's parked outside," Bateman voiced, standing in the doorway of the bar.

There was only one reason I went. I don't think it was the fact that I was drunk or that I had an overwhelming desire to go to the club. Rather, it was the second time on the holiday that I accepted a lift with a complete stranger whose car was most definitely red. I wasn't going to be cowed by Brenda's crank predictions. Bad things would happen? As far as I was concerned, they were happening already.

The club, over two miles away from the bar, was called Ups 'n' Downs, and from what I can remember it was small and our arrival doubled the total occupancy, probably due to the fact that it was a Tuesday evening and was in the middle of nowhere. I'm not sure how much earlier I left than Eric and Bateman, but it must have been the exact amount of time it took for me to walk back to the motel, as I arrived there just as Bateman and Eric did likewise in Eric's car.

"Thanks for a good night, Luke," Eric said as Bateman stood by the wing of the car holding the door wide open. "I'm off back to Connecticut now, buddy."

Bateman, by now in a horribly drunken state, then returned to the front passenger seat of the car and slammed the door. "I'm going, too."

After I explained several times to Bateman that Connecticut was a completely different state and not a bigger and better nightclub further down the road, he reluctantly got out. Eric locked the door so Bateman couldn't change his mind, and sped off. By now Bateman had been attracted to one of the rooms on the ground floor by the reception desk, as there appeared to be some kind of party in progress. I returned to our room and closed the door, peeping through the window. I could see Bateman swaying outside the other room, talking to a few of the party guests who stood in the doorway, neither inviting him in nor asking him to leave. As I stripped down to my boxer shorts and collapsed into bed, I knew it was only a matter of time until Bateman returned to the room.

In fact, it was a good hour or so before he did . . . under the supervision of the Boston police. I was dressed in just boxer shorts and a T-shirt, my goatee on full display. Surely I was in for it.

"Take him in and keep him here or we'll be back," said the cop, who was holding a shoeless Bateman.

"OK, Officer, I will," I replied as the cop and his partner began to walk away down the steps. Then they stopped.

"Just one more thing," the officer said, turning his face to me.

I held my breath. Was this the moment when I would be arrested? "Have a nice night, sir."

Bateman, who couldn't remember anything of his actions the following morning, said I could have dreamt the entire thing. The prospect of having dreamt about a drunken Bateman was alarming, but his suspicions were laid to rest when we found his shoes outside the door.

Boston, as I was told by the many Americans I had met en route, was a city I would love. "They're like you" and "they talk like you there" were generally the main reasons given. In reality Boston was a joy of a town and one of those rare Americans cities that were built before the invention of the car. Until 1755, Boston was the biggest city in America, and even now walking around the narrow streets is a fascinating insight into America's beginnings. The city is even better explored with a small goatee on your face.

Obviously, a city steeped in history, culture, and life cannot be evaluated simply by those merits alone. Oh, no. In Bateman's and my eyes, of course, it must have pleasant tramps. Put to the test, Boston emerged faultless when I told one beggar I had no spare change, to which he replied, "That's OK. God bless you, man." St. Louis had finally been relegated to the lower leagues.

There were only two things Bateman wanted to do in Boston and, surprisingly, neither of them involved Hooters or the visiting thereof. Instead, Bateman wanted to visit the bar that was pictured in the opening credits to the sitcom *Cheers*. Even more alarmingly, he wanted to get a tattoo.

"A tattoo? Why do you want to get a tattoo?" I asked.

"Because I'm in the mood."

I wasn't quite sure as to what kind of "mood" someone has to be in to have their skin permanently painted; I was happy if I could just show my goatee a good time.

"Right. We'll go to the *Cheers* bar first, though, yeah?"

What I didn't know about Boston was that there are two *Cheers* bars. One is the bar featured in the opening credits of the television series, and the other was made after the success of the sitcom, its interior made to look exactly like it does in the programme. I'd actually seen very few episodes of *Cheers* and would barely notice any imperfections in the bar's appearance, but we both opted for the first bar, where the goatee could enjoy its crowning moment.

The *Cheers* bar looked exactly as it appeared in the opening credits, and a Dutch couple were already outside snapping pictures of themselves under the yellow domed awnings and the *Cheers* sign, which shook gently in the wind. Downstairs in the bar I was sadly disappointed. It wasn't because of the fact that the bar was littered with the obligatory *Cheers* paraphernalia or because the drinks were quite high-priced. It was because nobody knew my name—seemingly not even Bateman, who was still showing mental repercussions from the previous night. After a quick pint, which, and I quote, Bateman had to "battle through," we purchased two souvenir pint glasses and made our way to the local information hut, where Bateman could enquire as to where he could have a tattoo done. In what was likely a Boston information centre first, Bateman quietly approached the desk and asked where he could get a tattoo similar to George Clooney's in the film *From Dusk till Dawn*. The un-tattooed Boston information guide did what anyone else would: she asked the guide next to her, who did have some body art, where he'd had his done.

After double-checking its position on the map, the clerk sent us in the direction of the city's excellent subway system to take a train from the centre of Boston across the Charles River and into Cambridge, where Harvard University's campus was located. Only a street away from where seven U.S. presidents, fifty Nobel Prize winners, and countless number of political leaders, poets, and writers had graduated from one of the most prestigious universities in the world, Bateman had arrived simply to get his skin painted. Unfortunately for him, the tattooist was fully booked, and the design Bateman had requested would have taken over three hours to perform.

Slightly downbeat and vowing that he'd "get it done one day," Bateman and I returned to our motel room. Boston may have been a disappointment for him, but I had managed to successfully break seven laws in a row—a record that I was sure would come to an end at some point. In the bathroom, as I drew the shaver close to my face to finally remove the ginger goatee that had sat there for the past few weeks, I wasn't quite sure if I truly wanted to remove it. On one hand, it had helped me break my fifteenth law and had brought me to the startling heights of seven laws in a row. On the other hand, it was ginger. Decision made. But as the hairs washed away down the sink and out of my life and I studied my face in the mirror, I couldn't help miss what I had now lost, and I couldn't help feeling ever so naked without it.

21

To make way for improvements and to deal with greater demand, over time everything grows in size and stature to accommodate the needs of the people. It comes as no surprise to discover that the wing of a Boeing 747 is longer than the world's first-ever flight and that for well over two hundred years Lincoln Cathedral was the tallest building in the world, even though nowadays it wouldn't make it into the top one thousand.

So why, when everything else has grown to astronomical scales, does the bathtub remain at a size where only certain parts of your body can be washed at a time? When the legs are in, the upper body is out, and when your chest is totally submerged, your knees rise into the air and brave the temperatures of the bathroom. Surely some bright spark can create a bath that is seven feet long, which would accommodate most human life on earth and get back at dwarves and midgets, who must be feeling pretty smug about the entire bathtub crisis.

I put the bath question to Bateman as we pulled into Longmeadow, Massachusetts, because my arrival there saw the first time since I grew too tall to fit in a bath properly that I was glad tubs were the standard 5 feet. In Longmeadow it is illegal for two men to carry a bathtub across the village green, and it wasn't so much the carrying that I was concerned about. I knew I wasn't going to simply find one lying around, so if I really wanted to break the law I was going to need to transport it to the green somehow.

"Right, Bateman. It's simple. We get a bathtub from somewhere, carry it over the village green, and we're done. It's a good job you're here. The law states two men," I said confidently.

Although it was never going to be that easy, was it? Breaking laws never was. However simple they appeared on paper, something would always happen and ruin the flow. In Spartanburg it had been our inability to find the cemetery; the nonexistent sale of kites almost scuppered me in Washington; the fact that no girl wanted to waste five minutes of missing out on the delights of Fontanelle meant certain failure there as well.

My first impressions of Longmeadow were not ones that inspired me with a great deal of hope. The village green was there all right, but only one single shop could be seen. In a town of over 15,000 I knew there would be more than one retailer, but to have just the one around the town's focal point seemed very strange indeed. The shop, Spa on the Green, however, did sound more than encouraging in the bathtub department until I approached its front doors and realised it was in fact a doctor's surgery that offered organic skin care and body treatments; from what I'm sure I saw printed in the window of the building, Dr. Glen S. Brooks was a plastic surgeon. How very odd.

With no other shops in sight, Bateman and I headed across the green and strolled up the sidewalk. The town hall (which was similar to just a normal home), a school, and the First Church of Christ all stood on a green that was picturesque in appearance but oddly devoid of people. I needed to find a store where I could borrow a bathtub, and so I needed a library to find a store. Longmeadow, though, is a town where the buildings aren't readily identifiable from their looks. Other towns' buildings would be easily identifiable from pillars or clock towers, but not here. In Longmeadow the town hall is known as "the building with the big white door" and the school is "the building where all the kids are going"; they have no distinguishable features to separate them from others. As we stopped the only person we saw, a small boy on his bike, and asked him where the library was, I wasn't surprised by his response: "It's the big building at the end with the green windows."

The Richard Salter Storrs Library, a big white building with the promised green windows, allowed me to use their Internet facilities, and I browsed the online Longmeadow business directory. Under "Home Improvements" there were many painting and decorating services, my favourite being the cleverly named Odd Jobs at Odd Prices. None of them sounded as if they sold bathtubs or had any I could borrow. Under "Hardware—Retail," however, there was one business that might be able to assist me.

We drove to Brightwood Hardware, a good mile from the lonely expanse of the town green. It stood in a tiny area of shops that was absolutely bursting with activity. One man was already in the hardware shop, and a lady was loading some goods into the back of her car as a child rode past us both on his bike. Compared to the green, the area was bursting with activity.

Although the gentleman who owned the store didn't sell bathtubs, he did know a place where I could drive to purchase one. After he had discovered that I wasn't from around the Longmeadow area and actually lived in the UK—to settle any kind of confusion, I just said I was from London—he began to explain to me where I could find Bay State Plumbing and Heating Supply. After he had drawn me a rather indecipherable map, I thanked him for his time and, only remembering that he said something about an interstate, that is where I headed.

Just north of Longmeadow, not far from the exit off I-91, Bay State Plumbing and Heating Supply is in just one of the thirty or so Springfields you can find throughout America. The store was one of those pleasant shopping environments where the products are laid out with special lighting and where plastic fruit is used to aid their appearance and help sell the products. The numerous bathtubs accented with Greek-style golden taps made me aware that this wasn't the type of shop that was simply going to allow me to borrow a tub for an hour.

"Can I help you, sir?" came a voice from behind an Elizabethan-style Jacuzzi. It emanated from a woman sitting behind a desk filled with bathroom brochures.

"Um, yes. I was wondering if you had any smaller bathtubs. All the ones here seem to be too luxurious and grand for what I was looking for."

"Yes, of course, sir. If you would like to walk upstairs, there are plenty more up there."

"Thanks."

With the idea to now purchase a bathtub, somehow get it into our car, and walk across the town green with it before returning it for a full refund, I made my way upstairs in an attempt to find the smallest bathtub available. It certainly didn't help that our car was a saloon (no hatchback) and wouldn't allow a bathtub of standard size easy access. The top level was nothing like the ground floor and looked like a well-lit attic. The laminate flooring that surrounded the tubs on the lower level was replaced with a plasterboard floor up there. And the bathtub hunt wasn't the greatest of successes. Either the tubs were too big or were so outrageously over-priced that I didn't want to run the risk of having to pay for a bath I couldn't get a refund on. In retrospect I should have asked the woman on the front desk if I could give her $50 or so and have a tub delivered to the green where I could simply lift it off, carry it across the green, and send it back. But at the time, I thought I had a much better idea.

"Hey, Bateman. There's bound to be some sort of scrap heap or tip nearby where people dispose of their old bath-tubs. All we have to do is find it and bring one back to the green."

"What?" Bateman asked.

Then I had what I thought was a moment of pure genius.

"No, no, no. We drive around Longmeadow until we find a house that is being renovated or built. Hopefully they'll have a bathtub ready to install and we can just borrow it for a few minutes."

As I write this now, I can't imagine what Bateman must have been thinking as he stood there, slightly slack-jawed at the absurdity of my suggestion. Even a drive to the tip would still present the problem of transporting the tub back to the green and would be made far more troublesome due to the state the bathtub would have to be in to have been dumped in the first place. The second idea was pure lunacy, and Bateman was right to shake his head. Firstly, what were the chances that we had arrived on the exact day that the builders were working on the bathroom and were about to install the tub? Furthermore, what builders in their right minds would allow two English strangers to borrow their bathtub for an hour or so?

I was desperately in need of an eighth consecutive vic-tory, and since there were only two laws remaining after

Longmeadow, I didn't want to end the spree as I had begun it—in failure.

"That is the stupidest thing I've heard," Bateman replied, seemingly not sure whether to laugh or seek some kind of medical assistance for me. "Just give up."

"No way, this is doable," I shouted. "I'm not letting it end like this," I added, before saying a line I'm willing to bet had never before voiced throughout the history of mankind: "This is a bloody easy law; all I need is a bathtub!"

"Well, I saw a garage back there; I'm going to get a drink. Are you coming?"

As Bateman purchased a bottle of Gatorade, I picked up a pint of milk, but then spotted something much more attractive through the window.

"Sod the milk, Bateman. I've got a far better idea."

Outside was something I had only seen in cartoons and on television—something so typically American, I was stunned that I hadn't ever seen one in all of my previous trips to the States. Just across the road from me, seated at a tiny table, was a kid selling lemonade. This cheered me up completely, taking my mind off the bathtub fiasco. When I was growing up, a lemonade stall was the perennial image of how American children who were too young to wait tables or too lazy for a paper round earned a quick buck. I quickly dashed over to the stall with a fresh bout of excitement and wasn't even disappointed when I discovered that the lemonade for sale was really iced tea.

"How much is it?" I asked the kid who was positioned behind the pitcher and who seemed to be the stall's proprietor.

"It's fifty cents a cup. How many would you like?"

"Just the one, please."

He poured the remainder of the pitcher's contents into my cup. I gave him a dollar and told him he could keep the change. Standing with my drink in hand and not wanting to down it in one, in fear of throwing it all back up onto the sidewalk again, I decided it would be rude of me not to begin some sort of conversation.

"So, how long have you been out here selling iced tea?" I asked.

"About three hours."

"How much have you made?"

"About three dollars!" sniggered one of his friends behind him.

"Three dollars in three hours, hey? That's a dollar an hour. Not a bad hourly rate, that. Whatever you're saving up for, I hope it's cheap," I replied. Mind you, he had positioned his stall outside a shop—good for potential customers but bad if they'd already purchased a drink and would rather drink something that hadn't been prepared by a ten-year-old and his friends.

"Well, I'm pretty sure I'm the only English customer you've had today," I estimated, knowing full well that due to the total he'd told me, he'd had four other customers all day and, if they were all as generous as me, he'd really only had two.

"*I'm* English, aren't I?" he replied in a thick American accent.

"I don't think so, buddy."

"Well, I speak English. That makes me English, doesn't it?" he asked whilst looking around at his friends to back him up.

"No. I'm English because I was born in England. You were born in America, which makes you American. It's not that difficult. Although all Americans emigrated from somewhere else. I might be able to tell you where your family came from. What's your surname?"

"Jeremy."

"No, your second name."

Not sure whether to reveal such vital information to a man who had openly admitted it was one of his dreams to buy lemonade from a kid at a lemonade stall, Jeremy kept his identity a secret. Quite sensibly, he folded the legs of his table and made his way home with his friends.

"I feel nauseous and tired," he said.

I wasn't surprised, after only five customers and an empty pitcher of iced tea; he had probably drunk the entire contents of the jug himself.

Returning to our car, I had accepted that the lawbreaking in Longmeadow was, sadly, not to be. I was out of zany schemes with which to pull a last-gasp success out of the bag, and Bateman was running low on patience. I had at least fulfilled the lifelong ambition of experiencing an American lemonade stall, and with the warm conditions of the early evening I could prepare myself for what lay ahead the following day. I only had a day in which to master the fine art, and as I made my way towards the town green (where I should have been carrying a tub), I wisely used the time to practise walking on my hands.

22
HANDS UP!

It is a little-known fact that although California is the richest state in America, the state with the highest per capita income is Connecticut. Unfortunately, the state is not rich in strange and obscure laws. In fact, with the exception that throughout the state a pickle can only be considered to be a pickle if it bounces, there was just one decree that I was looking forward to breaking.

In Hartford, Connecticut, it is illegal to cross the road whilst walking on your hands. Although I had been practising for the task the previous day in Longmeadow, I was still not proficient in the art. Originally I hadn't planned on breaking such a law in Hartford, as I had read that the law pertained to the entire state, but then I saw a conflicting report that it only applied in the capital. Wanting the law gods to look kindly upon me, I found myself in the centre of Hartford on a slightly overcast Friday morning in search of the ideal place in which to cross the road.

It wasn't that early, but still, the streets of Hartford were strangely quiet. Very few cars sped past just a handful of pedestrians and countless shops, many of which were closed.

"Where do you wanna do this, then?" asked Bateman

"Well, this is the state capital. May as well do it at the capitol building."

Overlooking the city's 41-acre Bushnell Park, the Connecticut state capitol was exceptionally beautiful and looked like a Scottish castle with a Vatican-style dome charging up into the sky. I'd never actually been inside a state capitol, and, with Hartford's being the last we'd see, I decided it was about time I did. The wooden carved pillars and chandeliers that hung from the towering ceilings looked absolutely stunning from behind the glass windows—but the building was firmly locked.

"Never mind," I said to Bateman. "I came here to cross the road on my hands anyway."

As I walked away from the capitol's steps and down towards the park, I could hear a man offering his help as to how I could get into the building. Too far away to care, I simply shouted my gratitude and shrugged. I didn't need the state capitol; I could already see the place where the road crossing was going to take place.

The Soldiers and Sailors Memorial Arch stood in the centre of Bushnell Park and just yards from Hartford's historic carousel, which, like most things in the city, was empty. The last time I had seen something dedicated to the soldiers and sailors of a particular state it was in Indianapolis and came with the added bonus of a roundabout. The arch was tremendous, built in memory of the four thousand Hartford soldiers who fought in the Civil War, four hundred of whom had lost their lives whilst fighting for the Union. The structure, 116 feet in height, is made of brownstone from nearby Portland with terra-cotta accents made in Boston, and the arch stands between two towers like the entrance to some medieval fortress. On each tower eight-foot-tall statues depict the kind of men who left their homes to fight. What impressed me most of all was the fact that the arch was too narrow for two lanes of traffic to pass through, so a one-way system had been enforced, surely making the total distance of road quite easily handwalkable (and if that isn't a word, it should be).

You know, walking on your hands isn't as easy as it seems, and if you are equipped with balance skills similar to the ones I possess, it's nigh on impossible. The trick I'd learnt in Longmeadow was to straighten the legs and to allow them to gently lean slightly in front. Too little and you were back on your feet, too much and you had an imminent date with the concrete below. After six or seven failed attempts where the furthest I had travelled was two walks of the hand which equated to about three feet and, put in easier, digestible terms, was nowhere near far enough, it was time I thought about the crossing more carefully. As I stood back and cogitated about how success would be achieved, the small crowd who had been attracted by my antics waited patiently to witness my next failed attempt.

"We'll cheat."

"What? How can we cheat?" Bateman asked.

"Well, not cheat exactly. I'm still going to walk on my hands, it's just that you're going to assist me."

"How?"

"I'm gonna put my feet up on your shoulders and I'll walk on my hands that way. It's like a boxer being helped out of the ring. The trainers let him lean on them, but he's still doing the walking isn't he?" Bateman agreed to my tenuous idea and collected my wallet and loose change from my shorts pockets before grasping my ankles and placing them on his shoulders.

And so it was that, looking like two grown-up kids taking part in a very lonesome wheelbarrow race at a school sports day, Bateman slowly walked as I scurried nervously to the other side on my hands. We looked ridiculous—a tall, gangly individual with his legs at a peculiar angle resting on the shoulders of someone who clearly had never signed up for anything quite like this—and it wasn't long before I was tucking my shirt into my shorts and awaiting my congratulation from the crowd. After all, I had finally managed to complete the challenge—surely I was due some adulation from the people who had cheered me on when I was going it alone. Everyone seemed to turn away and return to whatever it was they were doing before they had been attracted to the Memorial Arch, however I don't think Americans look too kindly on blatant cheating.

Having came face-to-face with one of them in Chicago and having heard two children discuss their love for them at the San Francisco airport earlier in the trip, Bateman and I wanted to delve deeper into one aspect of America (other than its penchant for bizarre laws) that separates our two nations: its obsession with guns. With the end of the spree only being a trip to New Jersey and a monkey and cigarette away, we tore a page out of the Hartford yellow pages and made our way to the outskirts of the city to see if it was possible for us to use a real gun with live ammunition. Connecticut, whose Gun Code of 1650 reads, "All men shall bear arms, and every male person shall have in continual readiness a good musket or other gun, fit for service," seemed the perfect place.

Wolf's Indoor Range and Shooting Center is a rather daunting place to enter if you're British and used to thinking an AK-47 was a pop group. Its proprietor, Ray Sausanavitch, is anything but intimidating, and although he has an ever-so-large presence from the other side of the counter, he cordially invited us into his shop. "What can I do for you, guys?"

"We're from England and we were just wondering if it was at all possible to experience shooting a gun."

Ray looked disappointed and shook his head.

"Sorry, guys. You have to have a licence, I'm afraid. Some people from the UK shot here a month or two ago but they knew someone who did have a licence and so they signed them in."

"Oh, OK. Thanks anyway. We'll just look around if that's OK."

Ray, obviously not wanting to disappoint and with a similar philosophy to that of a game show host who thought no one should ever leave empty-handed, offered us a chance to at least see people shooting, and took us into a viewing area from where we stood behind bulletproof glass watching a gentleman who was shooting at a kind of target I had never seen before. The piece of squared paper, which bore sixteen concentric circles that created a spiral and decreased in size the closer to the centre they were, was rather more interesting than the pictures of swag-bag-wielding criminals I was expecting. One man who had hit a perfect twelve out of a possible twelve noticed we had been watching every bullet he had fired. As he made his way out of the range and into the viewing area, the man, who was in his fifties with short grey hair and looked less like a marksman and more like a university English professor, removed his ear defenders and introduced himself. His name was Barry Leeds, and he was indeed a university English professor, as well as a part-time shooting instructor. Bateman and I explained who we were, but it didn't seem to make the slightest bit of difference, as Barry called me Peter twice in as many minutes. After apologising profusely, he explained that his friend Peter would be meeting him shortly, and that was where the confusion lay. Until Peter arrived, it appeared, I would have to be his temporary replacement.

"So, are you guys shooting?" he asked.

"No, we need someone to sign us in, apparently," I replied with all the hinting I could muster without resorting to a sly wink and nudging my elbow into his stomach.

We followed Barry into the shop, where I discovered members could try any gun they desired, ranging from Colt .22s, Glock .36s, and Beretta 92FSs to other guns I'd never heard of before for only $10 an hour. Ray quickly took Barry to one side and asked him something while pointing in our direction. A simple nod of Barry's head later, our names were signed in and we were ready to shoot. And with Ray's generosity growing by the minute, we only needed to cover the cost of the bullets.

"Right, I can only take you into the range one at a time, so one of you will have to wait in the viewing area," Barry explained. "Who's going first, Luke or Peter?"

"Rich," I corrected.

"Sorry, Rich."

"Bateman, you can go first, mate."

As Barry took Bateman into the range I was joined in the viewing area by Barry's friend Peter Marino, who'd finally arrived to relieve me of my Peter duties, and we got talking on guns and the police's need for them.

"I hear all cops in England have a gun now," he said.

"Where did you hear that? Apart from cops at airports, hardly anyone has a gun. All they need is a truncheon."

"Really?" Peter replied in shock.

"Yeah, no one needs them because no one seems to have guns. Over here, the guns are out and the only way to combat them is with more guns. I almost met one in Chicago, actually, when I was stopped by the cops."

"Really? You're lucky. Cops over here are taught not to be accurate but to pound out as much ammunition as they can."

Bateman, who had earlier bragged that he would be much

better than me due to his experience with an air rifle when he was younger, hadn't done too badly apart from the fact that on his target, which was arranged in a similar sense to the scoring zones on an archery target and way much easier to shoot at than the target Barry used, every single one of his twelve shots had drifted to the right-hand side. I took the ear defenders and safety glasses off Bateman, and entered the range to fire off a few rounds.

As soon as the door opened and I entered the shooting range for the first time, the smell of gunpowder instilled my heart with instant concern for what I was doing. The range rules that adorned the concrete walls behind the fifteen firing ports didn't do much to ease my anxiety much either. "Rapid firing," "quick draw," "hip-shooting," and "hammering the fan" were all banned, and with my poor understanding of the world of guns, for all I knew I could have been doing one of those by just standing still. Then it was made worse by Barry, who chaperoned me into port thirteen.

Barry handed me his gun and taught me the appropriate way of holding it before explaining to me the two different styles of firing.

"Now, there are the single-action and the double-action," he explained. "One way you cock the gun yourself and the other you don't."

"Right," I replied, congratulating myself for not sniggering at the word *cock*.

"Have you ever fired a gun before?" he asked.

"Only once at the fair. It was an air rifle, and I accidentally held it by my face. When I pulled the trigger the gun's recoil almost broke my jaw."

"In that case we'll use the single-action, which means you pull it back yourself before firing. That way you get a more accurate shot."

"OK."

"Load your gun and you're ready to shoot."

Just for the record, I loaded .38 special cartridges into a 6-inch Ruger model GP100 .357 Magnum, which to my English ears sounded more like an Ordnance Survey map grid reference than the description of a firearm.

Lifting the gun tentatively with both hands and staring at the target, 30 feet away from where I was standing, I cocked the gun with the thumb of my right hand, which by now was both shaking and sweating.

"How do you feel?" Barry asked.

"My hands are shaking. I can't aim very well."

"They're shaking because you're excited."

"I don't think it's excitement that's making them do it. They did this in Chicago, and I certainly wasn't excited then."

Closing an eye and gripping the gun slightly harder, I released the first of my bullets, penetrating the target to score a seven.

"Good shot!" Barry said, not wincing too much as I turned around and almost pointed the gun at him. "Just ease off the grip slightly."

After the first round of twelve bullets, Barry brought the target back in. It appeared I had hit four nines and a couple of tens.

"Not bad, hey?" I asked.

"Not bad, not bad at all."

A second target was placed onto the mechanical pulleys and jettisoned back to 30 feet. By now I felt at total ease with a loaded firearm, and with the remaining bullets I managed to hit the ten another five times and the nine another four.

"That was really good," remarked Barry as we entered the viewing area, where Bateman had just learnt from Peter that he was something called "left-eye dominant," which was why he had sent all his shots to the right.

Back in the shop, I explained why I was really in America

and assured Barry that there would be no way his students would ever study any book I wrote—they would probably find a better use for it as toilet paper. Barry, it turned out, was the vice president of the Norman Mailer Society and had published two books he had written about the novelist. Ray then turned to a shelf behind him and produced a copy of the book, *The Enduring Vision of Norman Mailer,* by Barry H. Leeds, as if they had rehearsed the presentation several times before.

By now, Ray's cousin Dave Zienka had joined us in the shop, and Ray's young nephew Mark was studying a £5 note and some British coins Bateman had accidentally spilled while looking for money to pay for the bullets we had used. As Mark collected foreign coins, Bateman and I attempted to present him with one of every British coin, unfortunately falling short, having failed to find a twenty-pence or two-pound coin. Promising to post the remaining two coins to Mark when we returned to the UK, I began to question America's coins and celebrated the British system as the simplest to understand in the world.

"Why do you think they're better, Rich?" asked Barry.

"Look, I'll show you," I said, laying the coins we had just given to Mark out on the counter. "For starters, the American five-cent piece is bigger than the ten-cent coin. Why?"

"Oh, yeah. I've never thought about that," he replied.

"In Britain we use the bronze, silver, gold method, which everyone understands. Look: small bronze, big bronze, small silver, big silver, small weird-shaped silver, big weird-shaped silver, and then gold. All in order of value. Simple."

"I see what you mean."

In an act of greater generosity and in return for the coins we had given his nephew, Ray presented us with a Wolf's Shooting Range key ring, a medallion, and a golden dollar coin each—these are seldom used due to the fact that they were preceded by a silver dollar coin, which was similar in appearance and size to the quarter—proving my earlier point about the confusion caused by the American monetary system perfectly.

"It's illegal to have wire cutters in your glove box in El Paso, Texas," said Dave, who until now had only spoken to introduce himself.

"Is it?" I replied. "I decided to keep well clear of Texas mainly because they still endorse the death penalty. I haven't been to Florida either, for that very same reason," I added.

"Yeah, due to the immigrants breaking through the fences. If you were caught with wire cutters, they'd presume you were helping immigrants into the country and then you'd be in trouble," he replied.

As Barry and Peter left it seemed as if it was time we should be leaving too, and with that we shook everyone's hand and wished them our best. For only the price of the bullets ($12 in all) we had received the guidance of a qualified instructor, been handed a souvenir key ring and medallion, and had even been reimbursed two whole golden dollars. Not a bad day. Not a bad day at all. Guns in my eyes were still a scourge of society, but the people who were behind the triggers definitely weren't, and if the people I had met in the shooting range that day are the type of gun owners found across America, I felt safe in the knowledge that maybe the country wasn't in such a state as we have been led to believe.

The Connecticut Grand Hotel and Conference Center fit perfectly into the sector of cheap hotel that attempts to pass as five-star accommodation—the kind of place I love. Using a discount coupon book for the umpteenth time on the trip so far, I managed to secure a room for only $66. Most rooms overlooked the inside courtyard, which boasted fountains and exotic plants, and we were free to make full use of the pool, gym, sauna, and spa facilities. Just for that certain touch of extravagance, the hotel boasts a magnificent ballroom as well. But that evening Bateman and I found ourselves in the hotel's restaurant, propping up the bar, where the television was tuned to *Family Feud,* the American version of *Family Fortunes,* and were cheered up by the answers given by the contestants, who clap after every answer, however daft and inconceivable.

"Name a fruit that's messy to eat."

"Chocolate."

Classic.

23

New Jersey surprised me. I'd always considered the state to be one big suburb of New York, the place all of the city's workers commuted to and from each day. I thought its nickname, the Garden State, had been selected for its ironic qualities. But the view from the Bear Maintain Bridge is stupendous, due to the bridge's great height and the sheer elevation and gradient of the surrounding banks that fall perilously into the Hudson River. When construction finished in 1924, it was the longest suspension bridge in the world. Today it stands as a testament to time and still looks as new as it ever has. The different trees that line the banks present a patchwork quilt of natural Technicolour, which seems to find new and exciting colours to amaze the viewer. The Hudson below, after one final change of direction, begins its direct and lineal progression through the state until its approach into New York City, where it flows alongside Manhattan tower blocks before washing into the Atlantic.

Apart from the fact that the bridge toll was only to be paid by traffic travelling in the opposite direction, I was cheered up further by what waited for us on the river's opposite bank: the winner of *America's Greatest Roundabouts*. Not surrounded by traffic like in Long Beach, not used improperly as in Indianapolis, and serving no great purpose like the two I'd found in Salt Lake City, it was set in deep woodland and offered four exits. It was the fifth one of its kind we'd seen in 10,000 or more miles, and I was sure it was to be the last— that was, until we continued on the road we were on and saw another a mile later, one that might have been capable of pushing the earlier contender into silver position.

August was drawing to a close and so was the crime spree, and the law in New Jersey seemed the perfect one on which to end it all. Throughout the state it is illegal to feed whiskey or offer cigarettes to monkeys at a zoo. Possessing no spirits and having a smoker as my travel partner, it was blatantly obvious which of the two products I was going to proffer to the apes.

Sticking to a timberland road that passed almost no homes other than farms before passing a park with enough play and sport equipment to satisfy a metropolis' children, we finally arrived at the only zoo we could find within fifty miles of our motel that definitely stated monkeys were a part of its attraction. After the formality of paying the entrance fee, I was handed a map of the zoo and discovered, to my relief, that the monkeys were to be found in the exact centre of the park, as if they were the jewel in the crown of the zoo.

With no great sense of urgency, Bateman and I decided to do a lap of the zoo once and ascertain how difficult it would be to break this law. No sooner had I passed through the entrance than I was confronted by the cage of a Syrian brown bear, a sign that asked you not to feed the animal, and an American and his daughter who were doing just that.

Just so you know, the Syrian brown bear is closely related to the grizzly and is the smallest subspecies of brown bear. As it sat upright with its legs out in front of the rest of its body, I discovered that this particular species of bear feeds on plant parts and small mammals and definitely wasn't partial to the Cool Ranch Doritos being hurled over the top of its cage by the girl and her father. Rather hypocritically I turned away in disappointment that people would want to offer such things to an animal when the sign strictly asked them not to, and made my way further into the park before noticing that the bear was now feasting on an iced doughnut that had been wedged through the bars of its cage.

On the opposite side to the bears, the wildfowl lake was home to flamingos, otters, swans, and, bizarrely, a cow, which stood at the top of a tiny steep bank trying its hardest not to slip into the water. I was excited to see the aoudads, an animal I'd never heard of, but was disappointed when I discovered it was a North African sheep. The tigers and lions were in their cages, but when they weren't looking for food they lay on the ground and waited for feeding time.

"Do something!" Bateman shouted as the lion opened an eye, staring at the human in disdain before returning to his sleep.

With the wolves doing their very best job of hiding in the undergrowth and the fact that I couldn't feed the goats because many of the birdseed dispensers were broken, I felt it was time to lay everything on the line and finally end the spree.

"Right, that's it. Let's do this, Bateman. I'm gonna need some sort of branch and no people around me."

The reason why I needed a branch was because an additional fence surrounded the cage that the monkeys called home, which created a setback of about 6 feet before you finally came face-to-face with a monkey. Now, I know that offering a cigarette to a monkey is bad in itself. I'm sure whiskey would be worse, but I agree that cigarettes are not an ideal item to let a monkey get its hands on. But if you've visited Longleat or a similar safari park and are appalled by the amount of damage a group of apes can do to your car, you do begin to lose sympathy with the furry vandals.

"Right, I'm gonna attach the cigarette to the end of the stick and poke it through the bars until a monkey takes it from me. OK?" I asked Bateman just to check that the plan sounded as foolproof as I hoped.

"Right." He seemed convinced enough.

Maybe the end of the stick wasn't pointed enough and couldn't pierce the cigarette sufficiently or maybe it was the fact that I was too eager to put an end to the escapade, but the plan didn't work—the cigarette dropped into the area between fence and cage.

"Stuff it."

With nobody looking I leaped the fence and made my approach to the cage and was met by half a dozen rhesus monkeys who hissed and jeered my approach. Leaping and stomping angrily on the floor of their cage, the monkeys danced in rage as I quickly picked the cigarette off of the ground and threw it into their cage. It had been done. The cigarette had been offered, and I had completed the spree. I wanted to shout for joy and proclaim my achievements, but I had little energy. All I wanted to do was slump by the side of the cage and breathe a deep sigh of relief. I couldn't even do that for fear of being dragged into the cage by the monkeys.

Jumping back over the fence and checking that a monkey hadn't choked on the tobacco, I noticed that I needn't had worried. The rhesus monkey, the sign informed me, came from southern Asia and northern China and fed on nuts, berries, grain, insects, and plants. Tobacco, remember, is a plant.

And that was it. No fireworks, no tickertape parade or other celebration of any kind met the completion of the spree—just the noise of the animals surrounding me. Sure, I was happy it was over, but I realized I should have planned ahead and at least brought a party popper into the zoo with me.

Bateman, though, had a better plan. After over 11,000 miles of travel, staying in motels ranging from the abysmal to the moderately OK, he knew exactly where we should hold over our end-of-spree celebration. Why shouldn't we combine our credit cards? Why couldn't we stay in the only five-star waterfront hotel in New York City? We deserved it. Stuff it. That night we'd celebrate in Battery Park, overlooking the Statue of Liberty in our own $500 room at the Ritz-Carlton.

After a pleasant discussion about Bolton Wanderers and their hopes for a successful Premiership campaign, our taxi driver dropped us off at the steps of the Ritz-Carlton, where somebody took our bags and one of the helpful doormen opened the door for us. We were probably the first people in Ritz-Carlton history to check in wearing shorts and T-shirts, each with a crate of Budweiser on our shoulders. My motel coupon book brought about no reduction in the price.

Leo, a very friendly and helpful concierge, who's obviously that way because the normal clientele tips well, showed us around our room and received $2 for his assistance. The clean and superbly presented room had a fantastic view of the Brooklyn Bridge, Battery Park, and the Statue of Liberty, it even came with a telescope through which we could view the landmarks synonymous with the Big Apple in closer detail.

After taking some time to empty the entire contents of the mini-bar and exchange them with thirty-six cans of Bud-weiser (I know how much a mini-bar costs and I'm not falling for their game), Bateman emerged from the bathroom a little after three in the afternoon dressed in a white Ritz-Carlton dressing gown.

"Right, that's me sorted. I'm getting my money's worth and staying here until a minute before check-out time."

"They've got robes?" I asked in surprise.

"Yeah, there's another one in there."

Excitedly I ran to the bathroom and slipped into my very own dressing gown. I joined Bateman at the window of our room where, with the goddess of liberty as our witness, we chinked our lager-filled champagne glasses and congratulated ourselves on successfully breaking seventeen laws out of a possible twenty-four.

But it's just not that simple, is it? Twenty-four is a terrible number on which to end. It has no rounded quality. It sounds as if things are not quite complete. I'm pretty sure God only added "Thou shall not desire your neighbour's house" (or whatever it is) because he didn't want to leave the commandments at nine. For that same reason, Ali Baba probably hired his useless cousin just so he could have forty thieves and not thirty-nine. Apart from the fact that it is illegal to walk down the street whilst reading a book, New York City didn't have any appropriately ridiculous laws for us to break. Bateman and I scratched our heads, wondering how we could possibly break a twenty-fifth law before I boarded my flight the next day.

We had an evening drink at the Ritz's exclusive bar, Rise, on the fourteenth floor of the hotel. I paid $12 for a cocktail and could hardly taste the alcohol. We did enjoy the fantastic nighttime views of the New York and New Jersey skylines and the Brooklyn and Manhattan bridges. Tourist boats plied the river far below.

The following morning Bateman got out of bed surprisingly early. He wanted to make full use of his remaining time in the hotel. Still in the dressing gown he had slept in, he made his way into the bathroom like a man possessed.

"Rich, do you want a towel to take home?"

"Yeah, I was gonna take one of the hand towels," I replied.

"Right, then, I'll steal the other four."

Returning with the towels and a wash bag, Bateman started rummaging through drawers and cupboards, taking everything he could find that carried the Ritz-Carlton motif and placing them into his bag. He ended up having to steal an additional laundry bag to make more room for his swag. He crammed a shoehorn, a stationery kit, pens, envelopes, four leather cases in which the hotel kept their menus, and a few other things that caught his eye into his luggage. I was sure that if our room hadn't been located on the tenth floor, Bateman would have had a go at anything that wasn't bolted down. He even managed to swipe a leather note holder that he had found outside our room by the lift. I was quite envious.

"That looks nice. Can't I have it?" I asked after poking my head around the corner of our door to see if it had been replaced.

"No, it's mine. Just go down a few floors and steal one of theirs," he replied.

I set out to get one, but I had chambermaids watching my every move. I returned to our room empty-handed just as Bateman added the finishing touches to his own personal crime spree, stopping short at the television.

"Are you sure you don't want the carpet, Bateman?" I asked.

"No, I'm quite happy with what I have, thanks."

As we packed the remainder of our belongings—and the

hotel's—into our bags and began to make our way towards the lift, I noticed the receipt the hotel had placed under our door during the night. Day of checkout: August 30. It had been exactly one month since Bateman had received his speeding fine. Today, a warrant would be issued in the state of Wyoming for his arrest. If the fact that his luggage had doubled in weight since his Ritz arrival wasn't criminal offence enough, his bail jumping certainly was. And we had the piece of paper to prove it.

"Hey, that judge is waiting for you to show up in Wyoming, mate. That's twenty-five laws. Twenty-six if you're caught by security," I yelled.

"Really? I suppose that's it then. It's over," he replied.

As we stood by the lift, it seemed like a lifetime ago that I had checked into my first hotel in San Francisco with so many miles to travel and so little idea of what was going to happen. Even the fortune-teller hadn't helped. I certainly hadn't got into danger in a red car. I supposed that if her red car forebodings hadn't materialised, then her predictions about my strong character, financial success, and the two girls fighting over me probably wouldn't come true either. I couldn't get too upset about it.

I couldn't wait to go home and see family and friends once more. But for a brief instant in the corridor of the hotel, I wanted to do it all over again—meet the same people, see the same places, and break the same laws—though I'd hope the second time to succeed at more than eighteen. My bank manager might not have been happy with the way I had lived the previous fifty days of my life, but I felt a strange sense of pride in my achievement. I would have suggested a final celebration with Bateman in the way we both would have liked to remember the end of a fantastic summer . . . but there was only one Hooters in Manhattan, and it was too far away.

The lift finally arrived, pinging to announce its arrival. As the doors opened and I began to step inside, Bateman swung his arm across my chest and pointed at the table to my right.

"Look! There's another leather note holder there, mate. Nick it."

Epilogue

Bateman still owns the summons he received on the day of his speeding offence. As far as I know, it currently hangs in a frame adorning one of the walls of his house. The state of Wyoming did not detain Bateman in the country. In fact, he left the States earlier than expected, a little short of two weeks after me, after his money and credit cards were stolen while he sat at a $200 VIP table in a Miami nightclub.

The roadkill game, though Bateman considers it a personal triumph, is still without an official winner due to the fact that an adequate and fair scoring system has yet to be adopted.

Only one of Brenda's premonitions came true. I moved house.

Acknowledgments

There are many people whom I would like to thank for making everything possible. Not least of all is my agent, Rebecca Winfield, and Gail Haslam's Transworld publishing team, who believed in me and who actually thought I could write a good book in under two months. I wrote *a* book, at least.

Before anyone else I'd like to thank my neighbour Lewis and his family for luring me out of the pub and inviting me to take part in their yearly game of Balderdash, which instilled the crazy idea in my head in the first place. I'd also like to express my gratitude to David Green of the *West Briton* for letting me write the story and to potential Pulitzer Prize winner Chris Mardith for being a perfect anagram of my name.

Special thanks should go to Arden Deloris for helping me kick-start my campaign when it seemed nothing was going my way. Despite his Snap victory, caused by the most definite bout of beginner's luck, I'm just relieved and appreciative that Arden was kind and approachable enough to take me seriously.

Thanks to Joye for sharing a pint with Bateman and me and to her mother for making sure I use my country facts more wisely in the future, and to Ann Traczek for correctly referring to soccer as football and for sticking up for me in a recent online forum when, for some strange reason, I was the subject.

I'm grateful for the welcome Bateman and I received from all the residents of Mineral Point, especially Joy Gieseke, Carole and Norman Rule, and Catherine Whitford, who were overwhelmingly helpful and responded with unquestionable generosity, and I'm exceptionally thankful for Lee and Jen's hospitality and cordial reception for welcoming us into their home for two days longer than I had originally planned.

For not shooting me in the face and instead very helpfully directing us back to the interstate, I'd like to thank the bulletproof-vest-clad police force of Chicago as well as Bill Stover and his son, David, who, like Arden, weren't initially shocked by my request and did all they could to make the lawbreaking possible.

I'd like to show great appreciation to Raymond Sausanavitch, his nephew Mark, and all the staff at Wolf's Indoor Range and Shooting Center for allowing me to fire a gun for the first time, and to Barry Leeds and his friend Peter Marino, whose instruction and assistance were invaluable.

Support at home was provided by my good friends Jon Davey, Matt Reed, Ian Parsonage, Sam Savage, my girlfriend Becky Brown, Kirstin Prisk, Tim Rice and his interested pupils, and Tony Parker, whose constant requests for pints have been the only bane on the writing, and to Sue, Mick, Tony, and Carl Reynolds, who will be among the very few people to have actually bought the book. And to Mike Dennis, Becky Watts, and Mike Underhill, who really didn't do a thing but wanted their names mentioned in the prose.

Obviously I would like to thank Bateman for accompanying me on such a bizarre escapade and for never questioning his reasoning for why he didn't just refuse. Bateman, I'm sure, would like to take this time to thank all the Hooters girls, especially Cassandra, and to thank Halifax credit cards, which have sponsored him financially and will no doubt leave him in economic oblivion.

My thanks go to Dave O'Brien for inviting me so warmly onto the Indianapolis airwaves and to his co-host, Ed Wank, for his similar hospitality and for having a funny name. Thanks to Angela Walker for being good-looking enough for Bateman to be smitten by her beauty, presenting me with the chance to have a good laugh at his expense.

And thanks to the proprietor of the only bar in Ocean City who had the good sense to accept our driving licences allowing us to drink in their bar.

No doubt I have unwittingly forgotten to thank numerous people, and for that I apologise. There was no deliberate intention to exclude people, and if any have been, it has been through a fault of *my* own.

Lastly I would like to thank my brother, Craig, and my parents for their love and support and for letting me do such crazy things.

About the Author

Rich Smith is a twenty-five-year-old journalism student. He is generally a law-abiding citizen, although he did once get a speeding ticket. Rich lives in Portreath, Cornwall. Visit his website at www.rich-smith.net.